HISTORIC
MARITIME MAPS

Author: Donald Wigal

Layout:
Baseline Co. Ltd,
7/1 Thanh Thai
4th Floor
District 10, Ho Chi Minh City
Vietnam

© 2021 Confidential Concepts, worldwide, USA
© 2021 Parkstone Press International, New York, USA
Image-Bar www.image-bar.com

All rights reserved.
No parts of this publication may be reproduced or adapted without the permission of the copyright holder, throughout the world. Unless otherwise specified, copyright on the works reproduced lies with the respective photographers. Despite intensive research, it has not always been possible to establish copyright ownership. Where this is the case, we would appreciate notification.

ISBN: 978-1-64699-737-4

Printed in

Donald Wigal

HISTORIC MARITIME MAPS

Exploration, oceans
and the art of ancient cartography

CONTENTS

I
MAPS AND EXPLORING
P. 7

II
DISCOVERING NEW WORLDS, WEST AND EAST: 1400 - 1500
P. 53

III
BEYOND THE NEW WORLD: 1500 - 1550
P. 99

IV
BRIDGING THE OCEANS: 1550 - 1600
P. 141

V
THE RENAISSANCE OF DISCOVERY: 1600 - 1700
P. 171

VI
SAILING TOWARDS THE MODERN WORLD: 1700 - 1900
P. 201

CONCLUSION
P. 232

NOTES
P. 240

INDEX
P. 242

GLOSSARY
P. 247

FURTHER REFERENCE
P. 249

LIST OF ILLUSTRATIONS
P. 253

CHAPTER I

MAPS AND EXPLORING

THE PORTOLANI: OLD NAUTICAL SEA-CHARTS

Maps, even those dating from centuries ago, influence our daily lives. They are one of the things that are part of our daily environment. Throughout history, besides its utilitarian function, every single map symbolises the period of time in which it was created. We are often reminded of the romance of antique maritime maps as we see them displayed in museums, or reproductions of them framed on the walls of private houses or institutions.

In a Vermeer painting a map may be seen telling a story-within-a-story (see p. 6). In plays and films maps typically set the period. In fiction they may be called on to remind the reader of a world beyond the story's setting. In Herman Melville's *Moby Dick*, for example:

> *Had you followed Captain Ahab down into his cabin… you would have seen him go to a locker in the transom, and bringing out a large wrinkled roll of yellowish sea charts, spread them before him on his screwed-down table. Then seating himself before it, you would have seen him intently study the various lines and shading which there met his eye; and with slow but steady pencil trace additional courses over spaces that before were blank. At intervals, he would refer to piles of old logbooks beside him, wherein were set down the seasons and places in which, on various former voyages of various ships, Sperm Whales had been captured or seen.*[1]

A map indicates not only the location of places, it can also help us see the world as did the people of its day. Each map is therefore a priceless snapshot in the on-going album of humankind. This is especially true with antique maps, by which we can see the world through the eyes of our forebears.

The Artist's Studio, c. 1665.
Johannes Vermeer
(1632-1675).
Oil on canvas, 120 x 100 cm.
Kunsthistorisches Museum,
Vienna.

While the map-maker's vision might later prove to be inadequate, maybe even incorrect, the unique truth it expresses tells a story that might not be revealed in any other way (see p. 10).

It may well be said that each map-maker effectively traveled in his mind vicariously not only to the envisioned places but also to the future. Each was sure, along with the aging Pimen in the play *Boris Godunov*, that

> *A day will come when some laborious monk will bring to light my zealous, nameless toil, kindle, as I, his lamp, and from the parchment shaking the dust of ages, will transcribe my chronicles.*[2]

One such laborious monk was the fifteenth-century mapmaker Fra Mauro. He was certainly responsible for bringing to light the work of several other mapmakers. By doing so he helped make the transition from the Dark Ages to the beginning of the modern era (c. 1450).

Mauro was part of the the generation that was at work during the very focus of these significant times, over thirty years before the famous voyage of Christopher Columbus to the New World in 1492.

Breaking With Traditional Church Mapping

Mauro probably went largely unnoticed in his monastery on an island within the Laguna Veneta (the lagoon that surrounds Venice). But his new map was destined to demand attention. It was large and round – which was unusual – almost 2 metres (6 feet) in diameter, yet still very definitely a map and not a global representation. It also included exceptional detail.

For the Asian part of the map Mauro took his data from the writings of Marco Polo. The rest was based on Ptolemy or his own contemporary sea-faring charts.

Mauro's extraordinary work was completed in 1459. That was the time when the plainchant sung in his monastery – like the plainchant sung in many contemporary monasteries – might well have been changing to the more harmonic presentations of such innovating musicians as Guillaume Dufay (c.1400-1474).

Soon polyphonic masses began to anticipate the elaborate styles of the High Renaissance of 1500. In that innovative environment, Mauro may have wondered that if the singing of even the sacred texts of the liturgy were being freed of their

over-simplicity, whether the Church's representations of the Earth might likewise be given a new and meaningful dimension.

Mauro's map did just that. By orienting his map to the south, rather than to the east, he broke with the Church's tradition. He no longer showed Jerusalem as the center of the world (see p. 11). Cartographer Alan G. Hodgkiss observes that 'Indeed, Fra Mauro's map can be said to mark the end of theologically-based map-making and the beginning of an era of scientific cartography.'[3]

Only sixty years after Mauro's map was completed, Martin Luther stood his ground against Rome. And in turn that was seventy years before Copernicus pub-lished his *Revolution of the Heavenly Bodies*.

More than a century and a half later Galileo would confront the Church with the shattering news that the Earth was not the center of the universe.

This was a restless time for the Roman Catholic Church that liked to retain control and preserve tradition. Also in transition was the Earth itself, as after all its surface was being "discovered". Its face was also becoming more clearly defined with each new exploration and subsequent map revision.

The Pisana Map, 1290.
Unknown artist.
Parchment, 50 x 105 cm.
Bibliothèque nationale
de France, Paris. (Map 1)

Just twenty years before Mauro's map – as if anticipating the need to get such forth-coming information to the world – Gutenberg (1400–1468) developed his revolutionary printing press. The first printed map in 1477 followed the first printed Bible in 1440. Both were documents that would support, in very distinct ways, the emergence of international humanism. As if to link early Church teaching to the Age of Exploration, Mauro's large circular map was completed at about the same time that elsewhere Leonardo da Vinci (1452–1519) was born. Also born at about that time were the future navigators John Cabot (1451–1498) and Christopher Columbus (1451–1506), and the future explorer Vasco da Gama (1460–1524).

Mauro could not have foreseen that these young men would in a few years be the great explorers who would indeed bring to light the 'zealous, nameless toil' of his and other pioneering map-makers.

Ten years after Mauro came to the end of his work, Machiavelli (1469–1527) was born: it was he who would eventually encourage the kind of creative effort in art

Arab Map Featuring Arabia as the Centre of the World, 10th century. Al-Istakhri. National Library, Cairo.

and politics that Mauro and other innovators prefigured. His was the individualism soon to be personified in the great explorers.

FROM ICE TO IRON: PREHISTORY TO 300 B.C.

Before launching into the choppy sea of knowledge that is the on-going discovery of our planet, let us briefly apply the theme of exploration first to the historical origins of humankind. The first thing to note is that in many discplines scientists once thought the epoch in which our earliest ancestors appeared was the Pleistocene or Ice Age.

In the late 1960s it was determined that the Pleistocene epoch began 'only' about 1.8 million years ago. For at least a century prior to that it was thought that the 'Ice Age' began several million years earlier. The academic juries may be out – as they nearly always are about such things – on how more modern studies will yet change the majority opinion.

World Map, after 1262.
In *Psalter Map Manuscript*,
London, Ms-Add 28681.
The British Library, London.

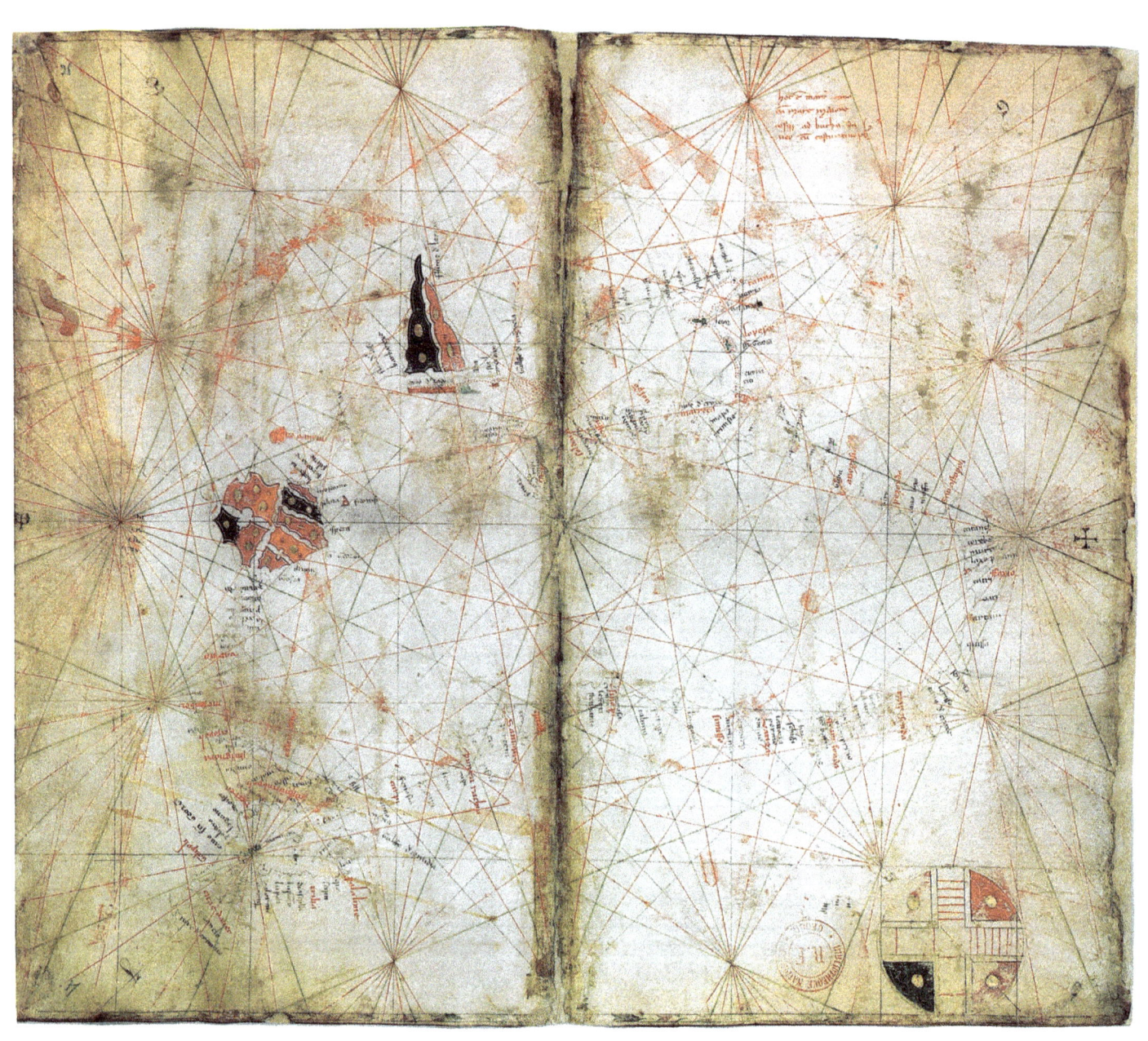

Atlas (Black Sea), 1313.
Petrus Vesconte.
Parchment, 48 x 40 cm.
Bibliothèque nationale de France,
Paris. (Map 2)

Atlas (Central Mediterranean Sea), 1313.
Petrus Vesconte.
Parchment, 48 x 40 cm.
Bibliothèque nationale de France, Paris.
(Map 3)

Enter Humankind

We know that it was during the Ice Age that the extinction of certain mammals began – but at the same time humankind first appeared some 500,000 years ago. Also, with remarkable speed and thoroughness humankind evidently migrated to the American continents, undoubtedly at times traveling one way or another by sea as well as by land.

Meanwhile, elsewhere on Earth other human cultures were evolving. As we skip forward 497 millennia – more or less – we see distinctive civilisations arise, such as prehistoric Greece in the Neolithic Age.

By the early Iron Age (c. 800 BC to c. 500 BC) migrations by the Celts extended the use of iron into central and western Europe. We might again presume that the transition involved some sea travel, if not yet trans-oceanic voyages. Iron would of course play a vital part in the making of tools, nails, and equipment needed to build the ships that would spread the more technically advanced civilisations around the world.

By the fifth and fourth centuries before Christ we see not only distinctive groups but also influential individuals, along with their works, who become known beyond their immediate circle of influence.

In Greece, for example, great leaders arose who would significantly influence all aspects of subsequent generations. Among the many great thinkers of the era were Socrates, Plato, and Aristotle.

A pupil of Aristotle was later to become one of history's greatest military leaders, the king of Macedonia, Alexander III. Although he would live for only thirty-three years, he was one of the few kings – along with Herod, the Roman-appointed king of Judea at the time of the birth of Jesus – to be called 'the Great'.

EXPLORING BEGINS: 300 B.C. – 1000 A.D.

Alexander the Great

During Alexander's triumphant thirteen-year campaign of territorial expansion that began in 336 BC, he extended his empire from Macedonia to India, and along the Mediterranean coast southward including Egypt.

Atlas (Aegean Sea and Crete), 1313.
Petrus Vesconte.
Parchment, 48 x 40 cm.
Bibliothèque nationale de France, Paris. (Map 4)

Nicolas Kratzer, 1528.
Hans Holbein the Younger (1497-1543).
Oil on canvas, 83 x 67 cm.
Musée du Louvre, Paris.

ALGEBRA MAKES THE WORLD SMALLER

For centuries, map-making, shipbuilding and navigation used only simple mathematics (whole numbers and fractions) for the calculations required.

The ancient Egyptians did not use symbols in their math, other than for real numbers; they did not use the abstract properties of numbers. However, problems such as we see in today's introductory algebra textbooks were nonetheless posed as far back as 2000 years before Christ by the Babylonians and, indeed, by the Egyptians. The Greeks, through their use of geometry, discovered and used irrational numbers five centuries before Christ – irrational numbers are real numbers that have a nonrepeating decimal expansion.

While they surely used mathematical principles, Ptolemy's twenty-six pioneering portolani were published eighty years before the appearance of the first book of algebra in around the year 250. Even four centuries before that, Chinese ships were built that were able to reach India, with or without maps.

Obviously, exploration could achieve a great deal without a knowledge of advanced mathematics, but much more would be accomplished as greater mastery of time and space through mathematics evolved.

Meanwhile, the development of algebra in terms of negative numbers took centuries. Hindu mathematicians first developed negative numbers in the sixth century. While complex numbers were not actually used before the late eighteenth century, the Italian Rafael Bombelli developed them in the sixteenth century, though it was to take another century before the theories were applied.

Calculus, discovered about 1665, applies differential equations to many practical challenges – in mechanics, for example. These complex numbers would prove to be essential in engineering and physics, and by extension certainly in shipbuilding and navigation, as well as in sophisticated map-making.

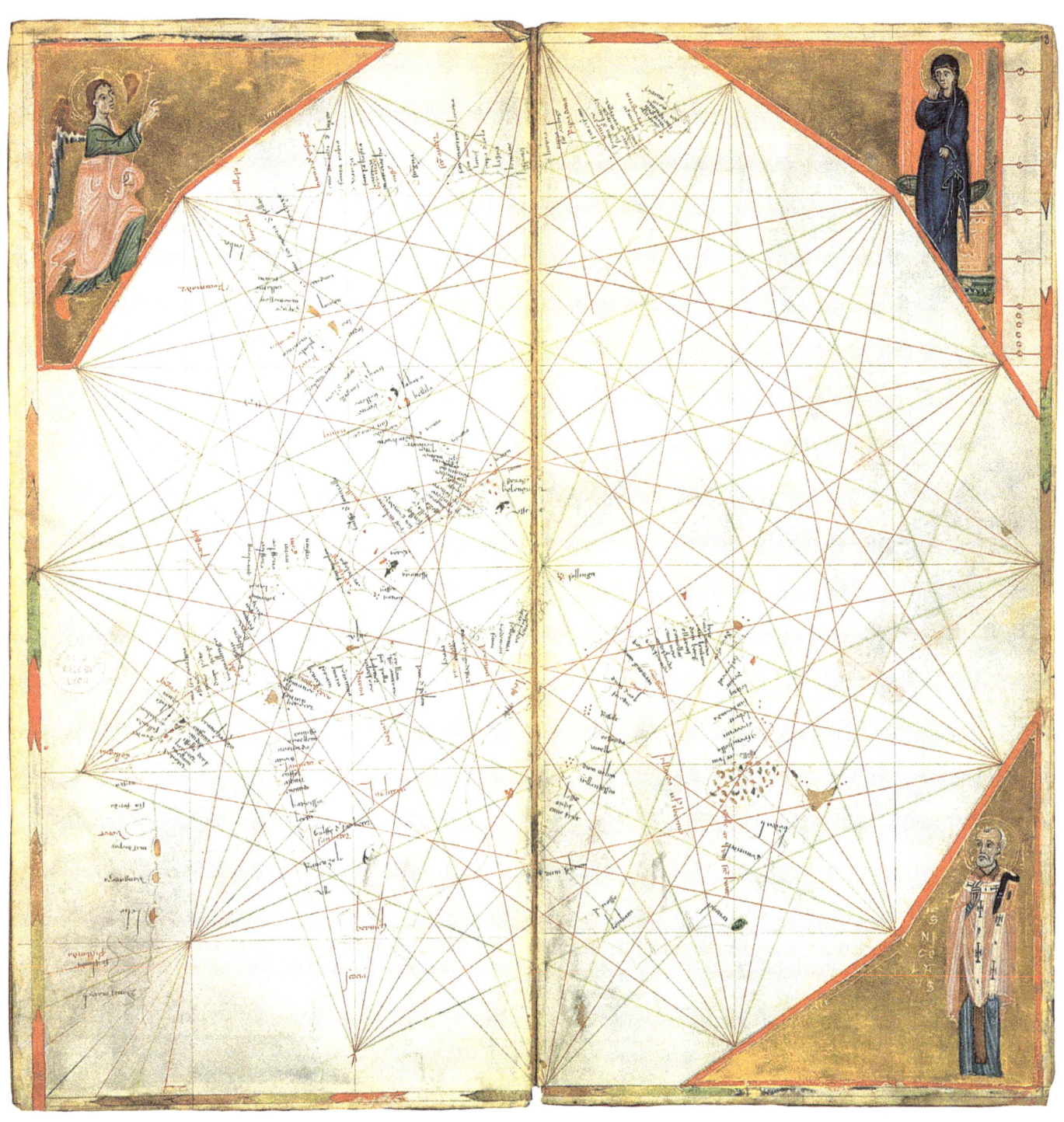

Because Alexander was a student of Homer and was fascinated by the figures of mythology, on his return from India he marched his army west through the desert of southern Iran towards Babylon – just as he thought great heroes of the past had done. He pressed on to Babylon and it was there that he died in 323 B.C.

Alexander was a military genius who used every opportunity to expand his territory by conquering everything in his path. Although his route of conquest was predominantly by land, he did assign a fleet of ships under his officer Nearchus to scout the northern coast of the Indian Ocean towards the Persian/Arabian Gulf. Nearchus' coastal exploration, while limited, most likely contributed data that would eventually be used in the preparation of the coastal maps of the area.

Alexander's western expansion undoubtedly spread Greek culture into Asia. It prepared that part of the world for the concept of obedience to a single King of a universal kingdom, which the Romans would build on for political gain, and later Christianity would accommodate to its aggressive apostolic purposes.

Erik the Red

A thousand years ago, the Scandinavian explorers known as the Vikings undertook journeys and left artefacts that remind the world of the contribution to civilisation made by these important pioneers (see p. 22). Some came to North America to escape the political unrest in Norway, living for over two centuries in peace and eventually establishing the world's oldest national assembly in around 1030.

Erik the Red, a descendant of Viking chieftains, established the first European settlement in North America. Around 981, he and his fleet of twenty-five ships discovered the land he named Greenland. He spent three years exploring the area. About twenty years later, Leif Eriksson (precisely, Erik's son), most notable of all the Vikings, discovered Vinland, later to be recognised as North America – although there is continued dispute about exactly where the initial landing or first settlement was.

In around the thirteenth century, as Iceland became a Norwegian colony, many of the greatest Scandinavian sagas were written in the Viking language, which is still spoken in Iceland.

Leif Eriksson

In his *Saga of Erik the Red*, Eriksson records the contemporary accounts of the grandson of one of the earliest colonists of Greenland. 'Our voyage must be

Atlas (French, English and Irish Coasts), c. 1321.
Petrus Vesconte.
Parchment stuck onto wood,
14.3 x 29.2 cm.
Bibliothèque municipale,
Lyon. (Map 6)

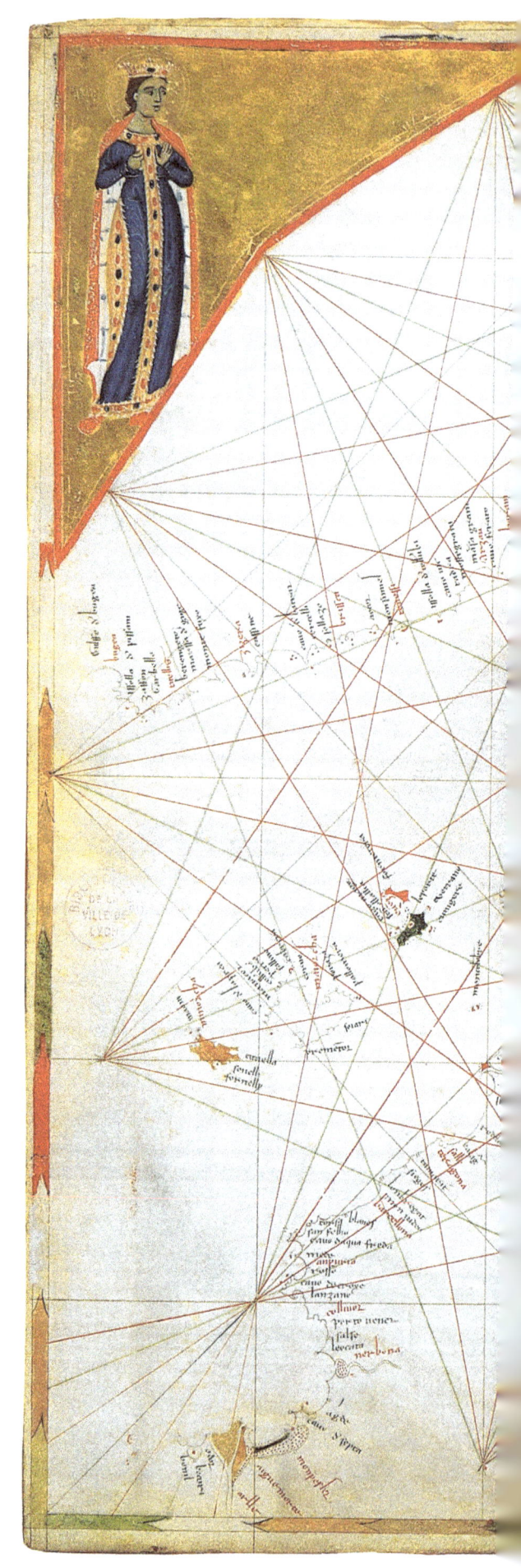

Atlas (Spanish Coasts), c. 1321.
Petrus Vesconte.
Parchment stuck onto wood, 14.3 x 29.2 cm.
Bibliothèque municipale, Lyon. (Map 5)

regarded as foolhardy,' the writer admits, 'seeing that not one of us has ever been in the Greenland Sea'.

'Nevertheless,' Eriksson comments, 'they put out to sea when they were equipped for the voyage, and sailed for three days, until the land was hidden by the water. Then the fair wind died out, and north winds arose, and fogs, and they knew not whither they were drifting and thus it lasted for [a long period of time]. Then they saw the sun again, and were able to determine the quarters of the heavens; they hoisted sail, and sailed that [period of time] through before they saw land. They discussed among themselves what land it could be, and [one of them] said that he did not believe that it could be Greenland. He asked whether it was desirable to sail to this land or not. It is my counsel (said he) to sail close to the land.'

Viking Nave and Marine Monster, 12th century. Miniature. Bibliothèque nationale de France, Paris.

The description of the coastline that is then described may well constitute the beginning of the first portolano of North America.[4]

In 1962, archaeologists unearthed the first hard evidence of a Norse presence in north-eastern Canada. L'Anse au Meadow at the very northern tip of Newfoundland was definitely a Norse settlement. A Norse coin dating from around 1070 was afterward unearthed at an American-Indian site in Maine. Moreover, 'recent scholarship suggests that Vinland may have been off Passamaquoddy Bay, between Maine and New Brunswick. Wherever it was, it was the birthplace of Snorri, the first European child born in America.'[5]

The widow of one of the sons of Erik the Red married the Scandinavian explorer Thorfinn Karlsefni, a Scandinavian explorer born around 980.

Oseberg Ship, c. 817.
Oak and pine wood,
22 x 5 m.
Found in 1903 in a burial mound next to Oseberg.
Norsk Sjøfartsmuseum, Oslo.

At the start of the second millennium, with three ships and 160 men, he attempted to establish a colony in North America, probably in about 1002, in what was thereafter called Newfoundland.

A collection of sagas known as *Hauksbók* and a section of another called the *Flateyjarbók* are cited as additional evidence, but it has to be admitted that these resources are mixtures of fact and fiction. We see a similar mixture again in the writings of Marco Polo, Columbus, and other explorers whose enthusiasm often influenced their documentation. Such imagination influenced their maps in general. For example, there are some unicorn-like figures indicating imaginedly weird native animals in a map within the portolano of the St Lawrence Bay area of between 1536 and 1542 by Pierre Desceliers.

Coming Out Of The Dark: 1000–1400

Marco Polo

Every textbook of world history mentions the Venetian Marco Polo and his amazing fourteenth-century travels in China. It is quite possible, however, that he never visited Asia at all. The accounts of his travels attributed to him may be simply very clever fiction. But it is more likely that when he was seventeen Polo did indeed accompany his grandfather and uncle, successful jewel-merchants, on their second trading journey to China during the last quarter of the thirteenth-century (see p. 27).

Either way, the descriptions of Polo's seventeen years of journeys are told in *The Book of Ser Marco Polo* – which for centuries was one of the most influential literary works in Europe. It could even be said to have laid the foundation for the Age of Discovery. Two centuries after its first publication, a printed copy was owned and studied by Columbus. In fact, Columbus made specific attempts to identify some of the islands he visited in the Caribbean as locations described by Polo.

While in prison, Polo apparently related the details of his journeys to a fellow prisoner, who conveniently happened to be a popular writer of romantic fiction. It may be that Polo merely heard these tales while sojourning in Constantinople or in the ports around the Black Sea – the episodes are not unlike typical 'fishing stories', openly exaggerated in order to entertain. Appropriate musical accompaniment to listen to while reading about his travels might perhaps be Rimsky-Korsakov's *Scheherazade* (see p. 39).

In a university dissertation on the literary styles exhibited in the works of Marco Polo, Enrico Vincentini (University of Toronto, 1991) notes that Polo's account of

Tribes of Danes Crossing the Sea to Britain, in *Life, Passion and Miracles of Edmund of England*, 1125-1135. Alexis Master and his workshop. Miniature on vellum. The Pierpont Morgan Library, New York.

25

From the Baltic Sea to the Red Sea, 1339.
Angelino Dulcert.
Parchment, 75 x 102 cm.
Bibliothèque nationale de France, Paris.
(Map 7)

his travels can be considered a 'lost' book, a book of which modern editions are no more than 'conjectural reconstructions' of the original corrupt manuscripts.

In any edition (or 'reconstruction') of Marco Polo's book, the descriptions are always exaggerated. Whatever he was counting, there were never less than thousands and even hundreds of thousands. Moreover, nearly every time hyperbole is used, the writer introduces it with such expressions as 'I give you my word …' or 'I assure you …' which is distinctly similar to the style of storytellers passing on obvious myths and legends. It is a literary device that was not uncommon to the non-fiction of the day, and of course had already been discernible for centuries in the scriptures of various religions.

How much of the Marco Polo work was the product of the writer's imagination – or the writer's enthusiasm – may never be known. What we do know is that the work inspired adventurous people for hundreds of years thereafter. Even map-makers, whom we might expect to be scientific as much as artistic, incorporated imaginary figures into their work, as seen in several maps here reproduced. These maps often exhibit truly vivid imaginations together with genuine data from scientific exploration. A serious study of them requires a specialised glossary and a knowledge of the history of their time

Marco Polo, 1857.
Engraving.
Centre historique des Archives nationales, Paris.

Catalan Atlas (Atlantic Ocean and Western Mediterranean Sea),
c. 1375.
Abraham Cresques.
Parchment on wood tablets, 64 x 25 cm.
Bibliothèque nationale de France, Paris. (Map 8)

Mediterranean Sea, c. 1385.
Guillelmus Solieri.
Paper, 102 x 65 cm.
Bibliothèque nationale de France, Paris. (Map 9)

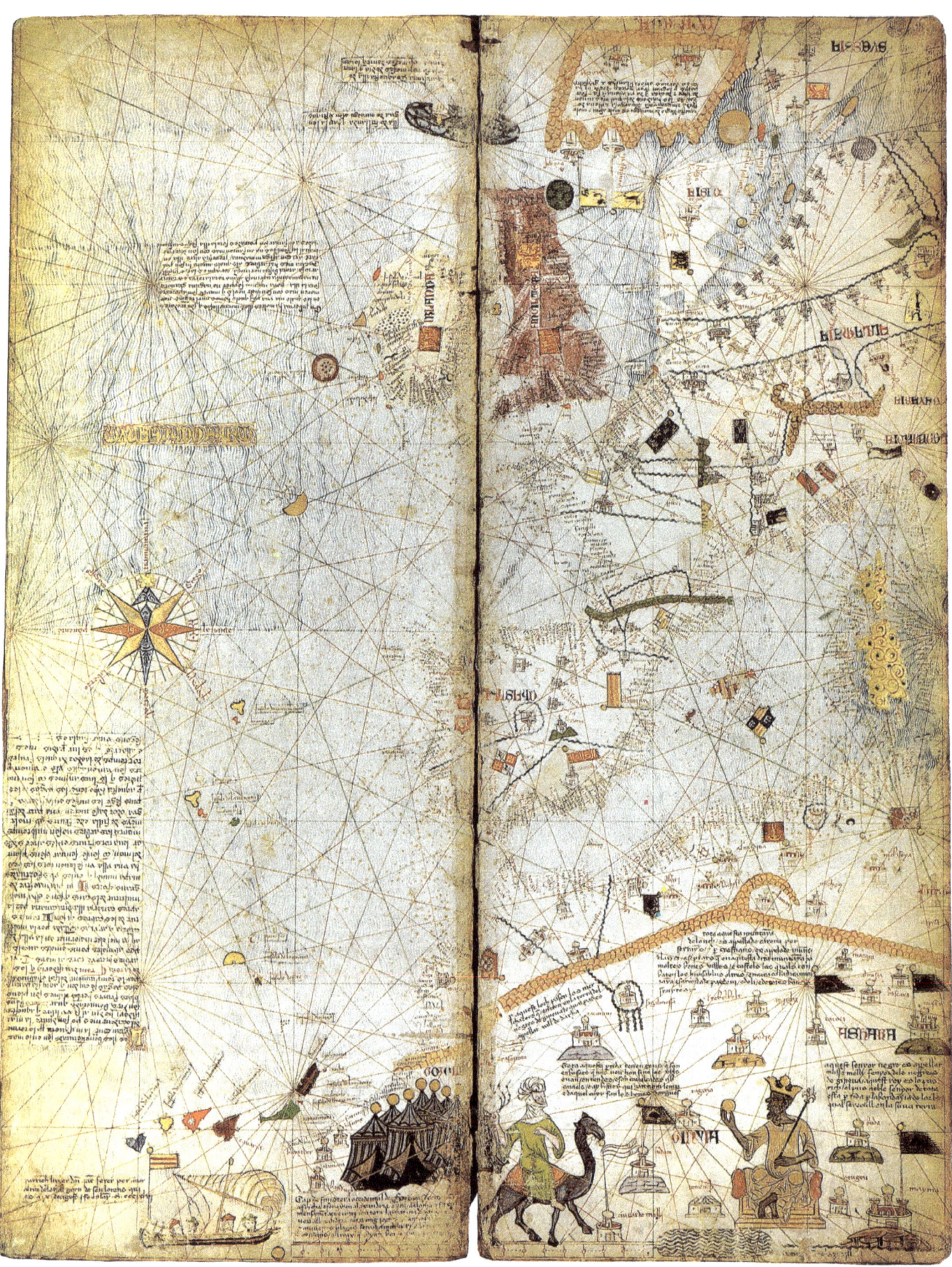

(as, for example, displayed in Ellen Bremner's university dissertation on the subject: University of Illinois at Urbana-Champaign, 1961).

The first journey east by the Polos was the also the first purely trading venture by Europeans in China. Previous visitors from Europe had been Papal representatives and religious missionaries who were taking literally the gospel passage 'the Good News must first be proclaimed to all nations' (Mark 13:10).

The Mongols, with their history of violent behavior, were deemed to be in special need of Christianity, even if it required similar violence to effect their conversion.

As with many of the great discoveries throughout history, what was actually found to be there proved to be a surprise, and in some ways more desirable than what was being sought. Navigators for at least three centuries after the Polos looked for new routes to the countries that they already knew about, not for new countries as such. It is not surprising therefore that none of the editions of *The Book of Ser Marco Polo* included maps, although ironically many details in maps for centuries thereafter were inspired by it.

The first expression of Polo's journey in map form came after his death (1324) in the *Catalan Atlas* (1375) (see p. 42). Many of the places named in the legend in that atlas appear previously only in Polo's descriptions.

The Franciscans

Two well-traveled Franciscan friars – Joannes de Plano Carpini in 1245 and William of Rubruquis in 1253 – were notable among the influential clergy. Their tales were less fanciful than those of Polo, but were often just as outlandish. They included descriptions of luxurious silks and other exotic artefacts desired by Europeans. Ironically, the stories brought back by these well-intentioned friars encouraged journeys by others who were not so ethically-minded. Soon Europeans returning from China managed to smuggle silk worms into Europe – risking their lives by doing so – in order to produce the much-desired fabric in Europe.

Spices then replaced silk as the most yearned-for imports, and the so-called Spice Islands (Indonesia) became the new favourite destinations for the trading enterprises (see pp. 40-41).

The memoirs of other Franciscan missionaries (Giovanni di Monte Corvino in 1294 and Odoric of Pordenone in 1318) supplemented the descriptions of China by Marco Polo, but their concern was again not to create maps but primarily to

Mediterranean Sea and Black Sea, 1409.
Albertin de Virga.
Parchment, 68 x 43 cm.
Bibliothèque nationale de France, Paris. (Map 11)

Venetian Atlas
*(Western Mediterranean Basin,
Portugal, Spain and Western France),*
c. 1390. Unknown artist.
Parchment on wood,
23.5 x 15.5 cm.
Bibliothèque municipale, Lyon.
(Map 10)

From the Baltic Sea to the Niger, 1413.
Mecia de Viladestes.
Parchment, 85 x 115 cm.
Bibliothèque nationale de France,
Paris. (Map 12)

convert the 'idolaters' and 'cannibals' to Christianity. Nevertheless, Monte Corvino was the first to report the monsoon cycles that were later vital to understanding sea-routes to India, as we will see with the pioneering voyages of Vasco da Gama and after him Pedro Cabral.[6]

Columbus described the native Indians of the West Indies as cannibals. His shipmate and friend from boyhood Michele da Cuneo said that they castrated teenage prisoners so as to 'fatten them up and later eat them'.[7]

Henry the Navigator

Seventy years after the death of Marco Polo, a Portuguese prince was born who would be even more instrumental than the Polos in advancing the Age of Discovery. He would become the fifteenth century's leading promoter of exploration and the study of geography.

Although the Prince came to be known as Henry the Navigator, he did not actually do any navigating on the pioneering Portuguese explorations along the coast of West Africa for which he gained his renown. Rather, he organised and sponsored them after several of his own earlier expeditions were financially unprofitable.

As previously noted, many explorers then and thereafter have been motivated by what some have called 'God, glory, and greed'. Henry the Navigator was certainly not alone in wanting to convert pagans to Christianity, advance geographical knowledge and acquire gold.

After a decade of attempts by others, one of Henry's navigators, Gil Eanes, finally rounded Cape Bojador (on the north-west African coast just south of the Canary Islands) in 1434. It was an area that was seen – mainly because of superstition – as a major obstacle between Europe and the Indies. In fact, Henry apparently told Eanes to either push beyond that point this time or to not return. Of course it was to prove to be only an early hurdle in a much longer journey, but new information from his trip was incorporated into maps by Grazioso Benincasa in 1467 [Maps 18–19].

About five years later the Portuguese colonised the Azores, which they had discovered in 1427. Expeditions then continued along the coast, mapping the West African coast down to present-day Sierra Leone. Unfortunately, the further the Portuguese went, the more they took to looking not just for gold but also for slaves to make a profit on as well.[8]

Orbis Typus Universalis Iuxta Hydrographorum Traditionem Exactissime Depicta, 1522.
Reworking by Laurent Fries of Martin Waldseemüller's 1513 Ptolemaic map for publication.
Biblioteca Nazionale Marciana, Venice.

Liber Insularium Archipelagi (Corfu), 1420.
Christoforo Buondelmonte.
Coloured paper,
29.5 x 20.5 cm.
Bibliothèque nationale de France, Paris. (Map 13)

Liber Insularium Archipelagi (Chios), 1420.
Cristoforo Buondelmonte.
Coloured Paper,
29.5 x 20.5 cm.
Bibliothèque nationale de France, Paris. (Map 14)

Michele da Cuneo, the long-time friend of Columbus, described the enslavement of the natives of Haiti before returning from the second voyage. 'We gathered in one settlement one thousand six hundred male and female persons of these Indians, and of these we embarked in our caravels on 17 February 1495, five hundred fifty souls among the healthiest males and females.' His journals go on to tell how about two hundred of these enslaved Indians died during the return voyage and were thrown overboard.[9]

Portolani During This Period [10]

The Pisana School

The Pisana [Map 1] is the earliest example (1250–1296) of a portolano. It is the oldest Western navigation map, and as an extremely early (and well known) map influenced all subsequent maps, especially those of the Catalana and Genovese schools. Although it may have been drawn up in Genoa, it is referred to as the Pisana map because it belonged to a well-established family in Pisa during the nineteenth century. It depicts the Mediterranean Sea in correct proportions.

The Early Genovese School

The portolani of the Genovese school (1300–1588) in this presentation [Maps 2–6] were directly influenced by the pioneering thirteenth-century work. In turn they substantially influenced the fourteenth-century Viennese and sixteenth-century Portuguese, Spanish and Italian schools.

Spanish and Italian Schools

Other portolani of the Genovese school include Maps 21, 23, 24, 26, 41, and 56. These also directly influenced the fourteenth- and fifteenth-century Portuguese, Spanish and Italian schools.

The corners of Maps 5 and 6 are decorated with popular patron saints of Venice, including St Nicholas and St Lucia.

Two anonymous Genovese maps of around 1500 [Maps 23 and 24] were drawn by the same map-maker using inks similar to those used by the Japanese at about the same time. The peninsular coasts from Vlorë (Valona) in Albania to the Pagasitikós Gulf in Thessalia are represented in the unfinished map of the Greek coasts [Map 23].

Marco Polo Leaves Venice on his Famous Journey to the Far East, in *Roman d'Alexandre*, c. 1400. Bodleian Library, Oxford.

Marco Polo with Elephants and Camels Arriving at Hormuz on the Gulf of Persia from India, in *Les Livres des Merveilles*, early 15th century. Boucicaut Master. Miniature. Bibliothèque nationale de France, Paris.

In the other map [Map 24] the coastlines of the Aegean archipelago are shown. It is oriented to the north-north-west, showing a new awareness of magnetic north.

Map 25 is known as *Cantino's Planisphere* (1502), one of the earliest examples of Portuguese maritime cartography. It represents the whole of the known world at the time, including recent Portuguese discoveries of up to 1502. The design was influenced by the miniature-painters Alexander Bening and Guillaume Vrelant.

The large maritime planisphere of Genoan cartographer Nicolaus de Caverio [Map 26] bears comparison with *Cantino's Planisphere* [Map 25]. It features nomenclature in Portuguese. However, it does not include information from discoveries after 1504. Its graduated latitude scale is an innovation not seen in maps before the sixteenth century. It is a highly derivative work. The same design and nomenclature are seen in the work at Saint Dié of Waldseemüller, who was responsible for the first oceanic map in the extremely influential 1513 edition of Ptolemy's *Geographia*.

World Map (detail), in *Atlas Catalan*, 1375. Abraham Cresques. Bibliothèque nationale de France, Paris.

The *Caverio Planisphere* outlines the shape of the Indian subcontinent correctly, but does not feature the Red Sea or the Persian/Arabian Gulf – areas the Portuguese had yet to visit.

The Catalana School

Early portolani [Maps 7, 8, 9, 12, 16, 17] of the Catalana school at Majorca (c. 1290-1330) also exhibit the long-lasting influence of *The Pisana* [Map 1]. Even later examples [Maps 62, 64, 65, 68] of as late as 1649 also influenced the Portugese, Italian and Spanish schools from the fifteenth century on, as well as the Messina school of the mid-sixteenth to late seventeenth centuries.

A synthesis of the whole known world is attempted in Map 7. Unlike previous maps in this collection, the nomenclature inland is important. On the map in the south of Africa is a region named as *Terra Nigrorum*.

In Asia, the Caspian Sea (*Mare de Bacu sive Capium*) is named. Three of the Canary Islands are specified for the first time. The Majorcan school, of which this map is typical, was to be imitated for centuries.

Map 8 may have belonged to King Charles V of France, possibly as a gift to him from King John I of Aragon.

On Map 9 the cartographer indicates in Latin that Europe is 'where Christians live'. Biblical sites and pilgrimage destinations are indicated, including the Holy Sepulchre (the traditional location of Jesus' entombment), St Catherine's Monastery on Mount Sinai, and Mecca.

The emblem of the Cornaro family, a contemporarily renowned clan, is shown on Map 10. Some coasts are drawn disproportionately close to each other.

The symbols of the four New Testament evangelists feature in the corners (clockwise from the upper right, Matthew is symbolised by a man, Luke by the winged ox, Mark by the winged lion, and John by the eagle).

Some important African warlords are represented. One of the ships near the African coast is that of the 14th-century Aragonese pirate Jacme Ferrer, who is represented also by a ship on Map 8. Sites are indicated where Arabian sources claimed gold was to be found.

That sort of information was usually closely guarded by merchants.

The impressive quantity of Joan Martines' output is seen again (as in Map 62) with his twenty-one parchment sheets that make up the Atlas dated 1587 [Maps 64-65]. His main source seems to have been the 1569 world map of Gerardus Mercator. This is a compilation of nineteen maps.

Mediterranean Sea and Black Sea, 1447.
Gabriel de Vallsecha.
Parchment, 58 x 93 cm.
Bibliothèque nationale de France, Paris. (Map 16)

Atlantic Ocean, Mediterranean Sea and Black Sea, 1462.
Petrus Roselli.
Parchment, 53 x 83 cm.
Bibliothèque nationale de France, Paris. (Map 17)

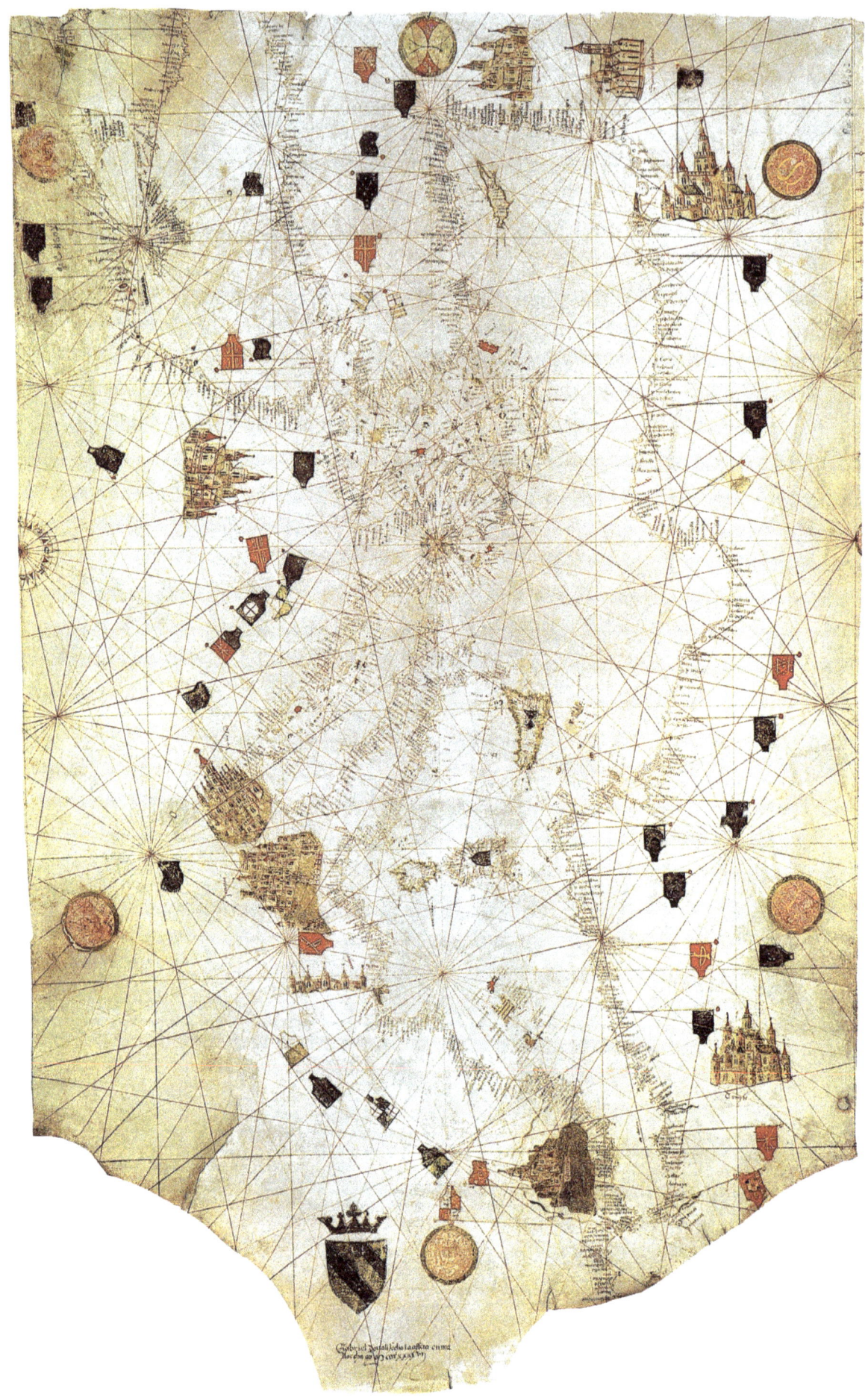

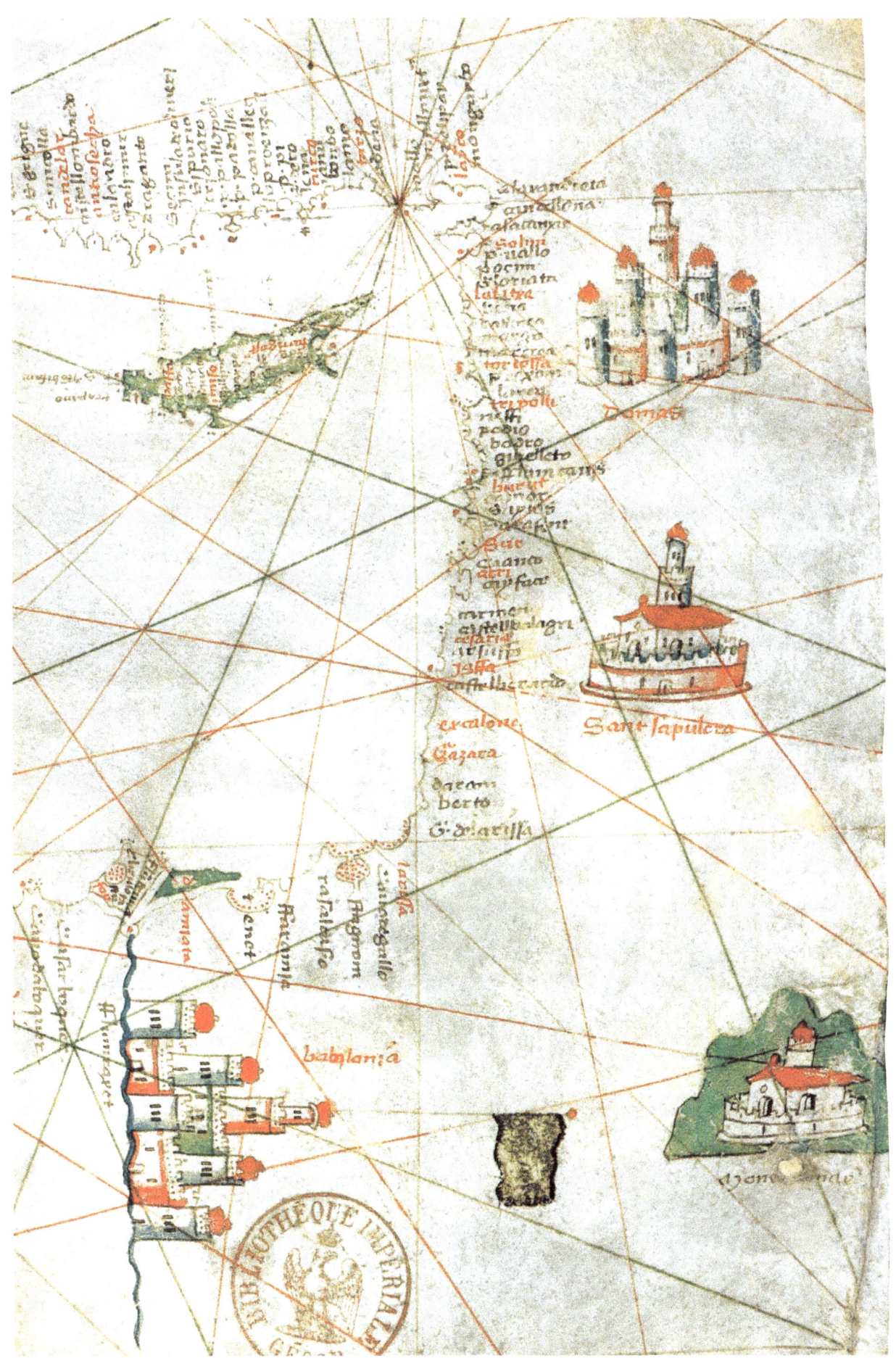

The maps may have been commissioned or intended for use by King Philip II of Spain – who at the time was preparing an armed (*armada*) expedition against England. It is Philip's coat of arms shown on the map.

The Viennese School

The portolani of the Viennese school (1567–1690) presented here [Maps 10, 11, 15, 18, 19, and 76] show the influence of the Genovese school. Their own unmistakable influence was primarily on the Spanish school, the Barbary Coast school in Istanbul and the Marseille school.

A close examination of Map 11 reveals that the artist sketched the outline with a dry point before drawing in the final version. The Black Sea is conveniently reduced in size so as to fit within the allotted space. The French coastline is somewhat cursorily dealt with, whereas the coasts of England are delineated in some detail. The map-maker endeavors to make light of such inconsistencies by presenting three different scales against which to estimate distance.

Symbols that were standard in medieval iconography are used in Map 15, including the red cross for shallows or sandbanks, and blue lines for lateral cordons.

As a young man in the mid-fifteenth century, Grazioso Benincasa kept a diary of his trips sailing across the Mediterranean and Black Seas. After losing his ship to pirates, he became a cartographer famous for producing more than twenty-two works between 1461 and 1482.

We noted above that details of Africa included in this atlas had only recently become known following the return of the explorer-navigator Gil Eanes. Yet in 1467 Benincasa was apparently quite prepared to use out-of-date information for the maps of northern Europe in his atlas, in which he included Maps 18 and 19.

A cartographer of the Dutch East India Company, Hessel Gerritsz, drew up his map of the Pacific [Map 75] in 1622. All the recent discoveries are noted, along with unique artistic tributes to Vasco de Balboa, Ferdinand Magellan and Jakob Lemaire. A world map, though very small, is also featured.

Because of its importance to the area, the Aegean Sea was often depicted disproportionately large in maps of the Middle Ages. The whole of the map produced in 1603 by Alvise Gramolin [Map 76] is devoted to the sea and its coastline. All the flags and shields show the crescent moon from Muslim and Ottoman iconography, for the archipelago was under Turkish influence at the time.

Atlas (Atlantic Ocean from Spain to Cape Verde), 1467.
Grazioso Benincasa.
Parchment stuck on card,
34.9 x 44.2 cm.
Bibliothèque nationale de France, Paris. (Map 18)

Mediterranean Sea, 1422.
Jacobus de Giroldis.
Parchment, 88 x 51 cm.
Bibliothèque nationale de France, Paris. (Map 15)

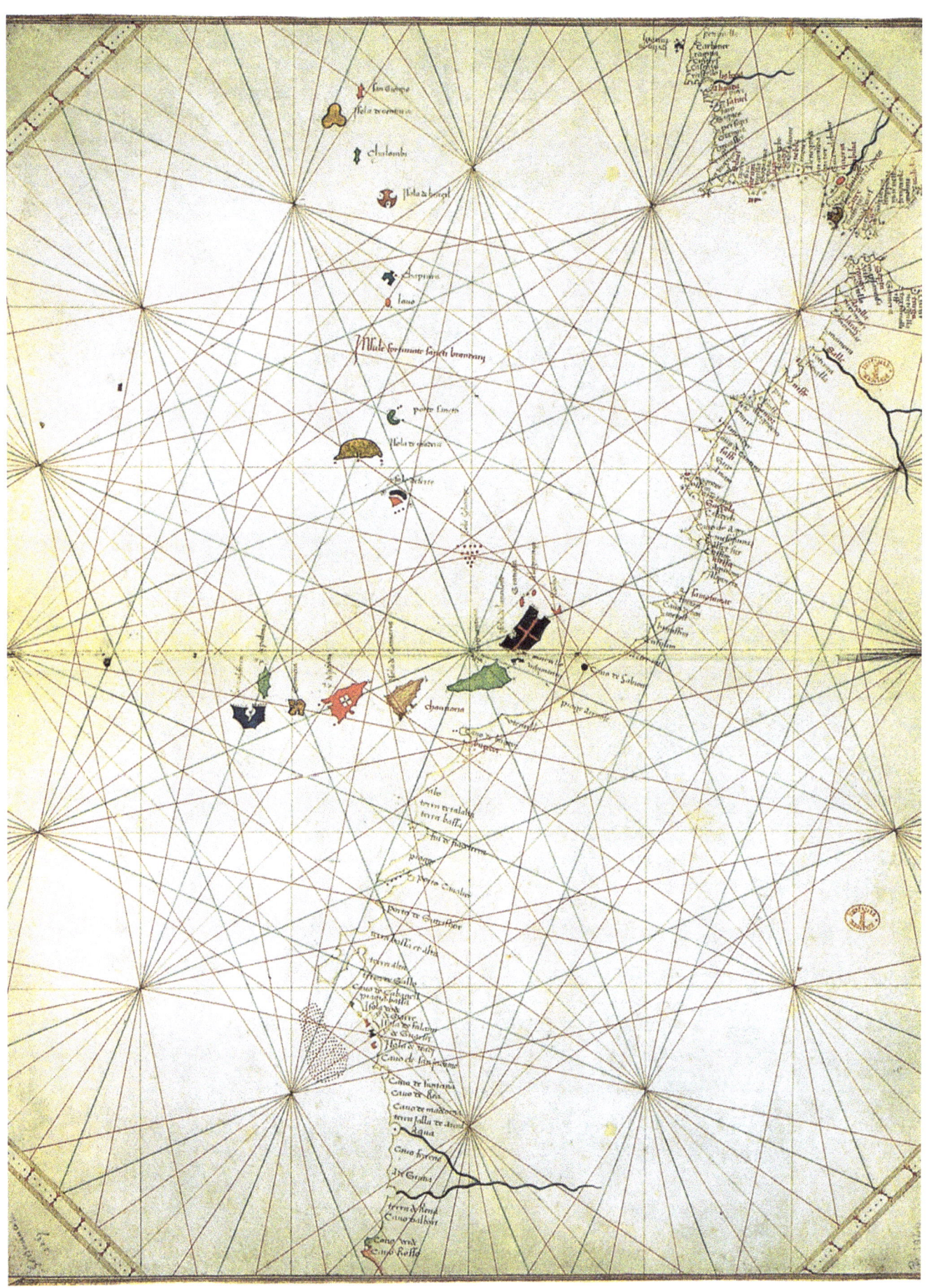

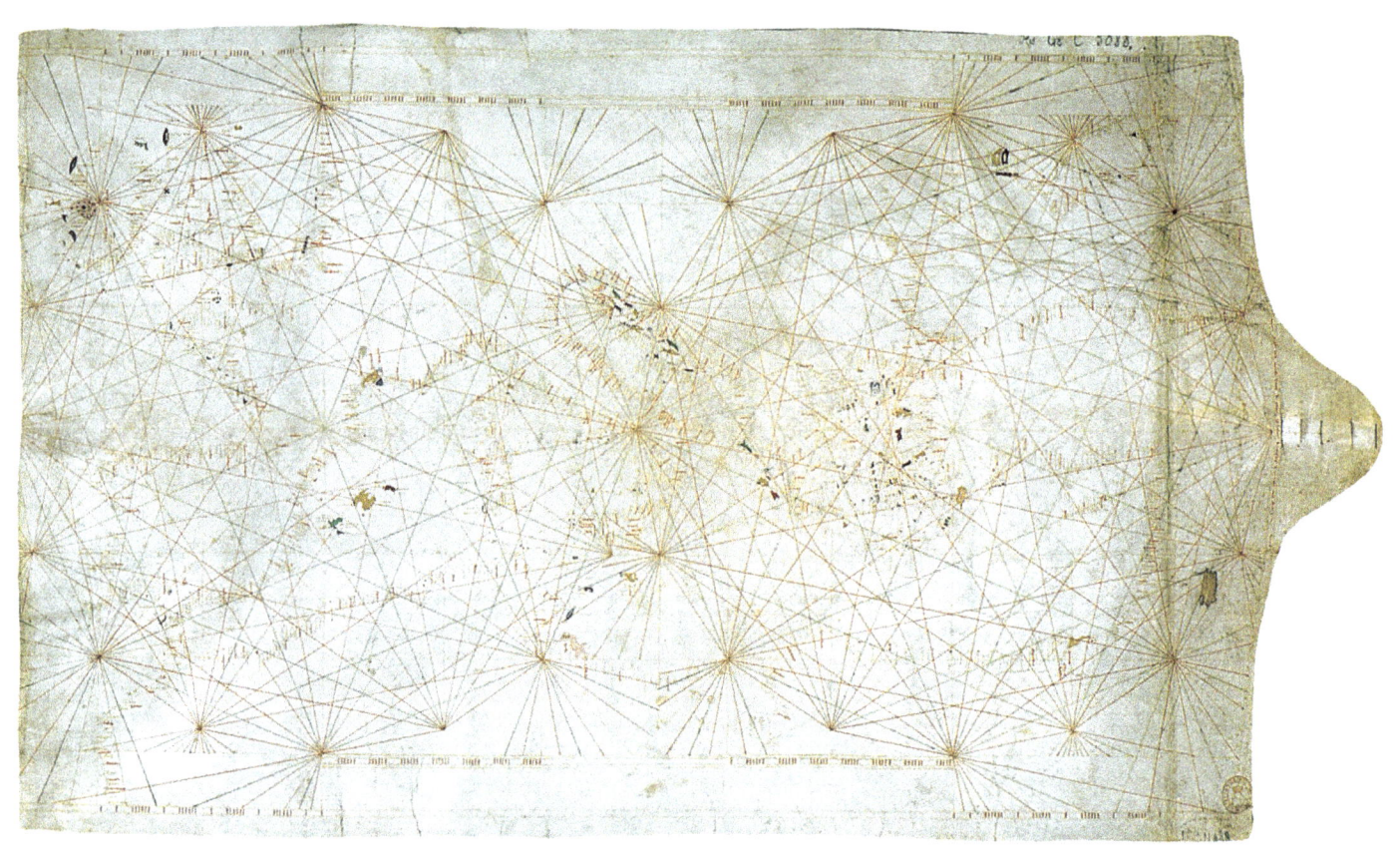

Atlas (Atlantic Ocean from Denmark to Malaga),
1467.
Grazioso Benincasa.
Parchment stuck on card, 34.9 x 44.2 cm.
Bibliothèque nationale de France, Paris. (Map 19)

Globe, 1492 (1847, copy).
Martin Behaim.
Parchment stuck on a 50.7 cm diameter globe.
Bibliothèque nationale de France, Paris. (Map 20)

CHAPTER II

DISCOVERING NEW WORLDS, WEST AND EAST: 1400 – 1500

SAILING OVER THE EDGE

We wonder what anxieties and hopes went through the minds of those daring sailors who first intentionally ventured far out into the open sea. They had no knowledge of what heaven or hell was over the horizon: the superstitions and religions of their day contributed to both their fears and confidences. And accordingly, the lands they discovered were given names of saints, and many of their ships also had names associated with religion.

Some, renowned for their apparently religious motivation, were later found to be prompted more by worldly profit – while conversely we have no idea how many mercenaries were actually men of intense faith. Yet they all risked everything as they chose to sail out of the sight of land, even beyond what they thought of as points of no return.

Many of those pioneers learned that it was wise to stay in sight of the coast, remembering and eventually recording memorable points. The tallest points and other notable landmarks were documented, named, and eventually became the sites of ports, giving rise in time to lists of ports and eventually charts and portolani. Reproductions of 100 portolani are presented in chronological order throughout this book.

Of course we today are on the same planet as were those pioneering navigators – yet, to be sure, we would feel as strange in their world as they would in ours. But we at least can transport ourselves back to the ancient world of explorers, navigators and their map-makers. In their maps and words we are able to see their world pretty well as they saw it.

Those men and women of vision in times past would surely be overwhelmed if they returned via some magical time-machine to the same locations today that they visited centuries ago. To better appreciate the world and times of these early navigators, we can use that same time-machine, putting it in reverse.

Aegean Sea, 1500 (?).
Unknown artist.
Parchment, 73 x 40.4 cm.
Bibliothèque nationale
de France, Paris. (Map 24)

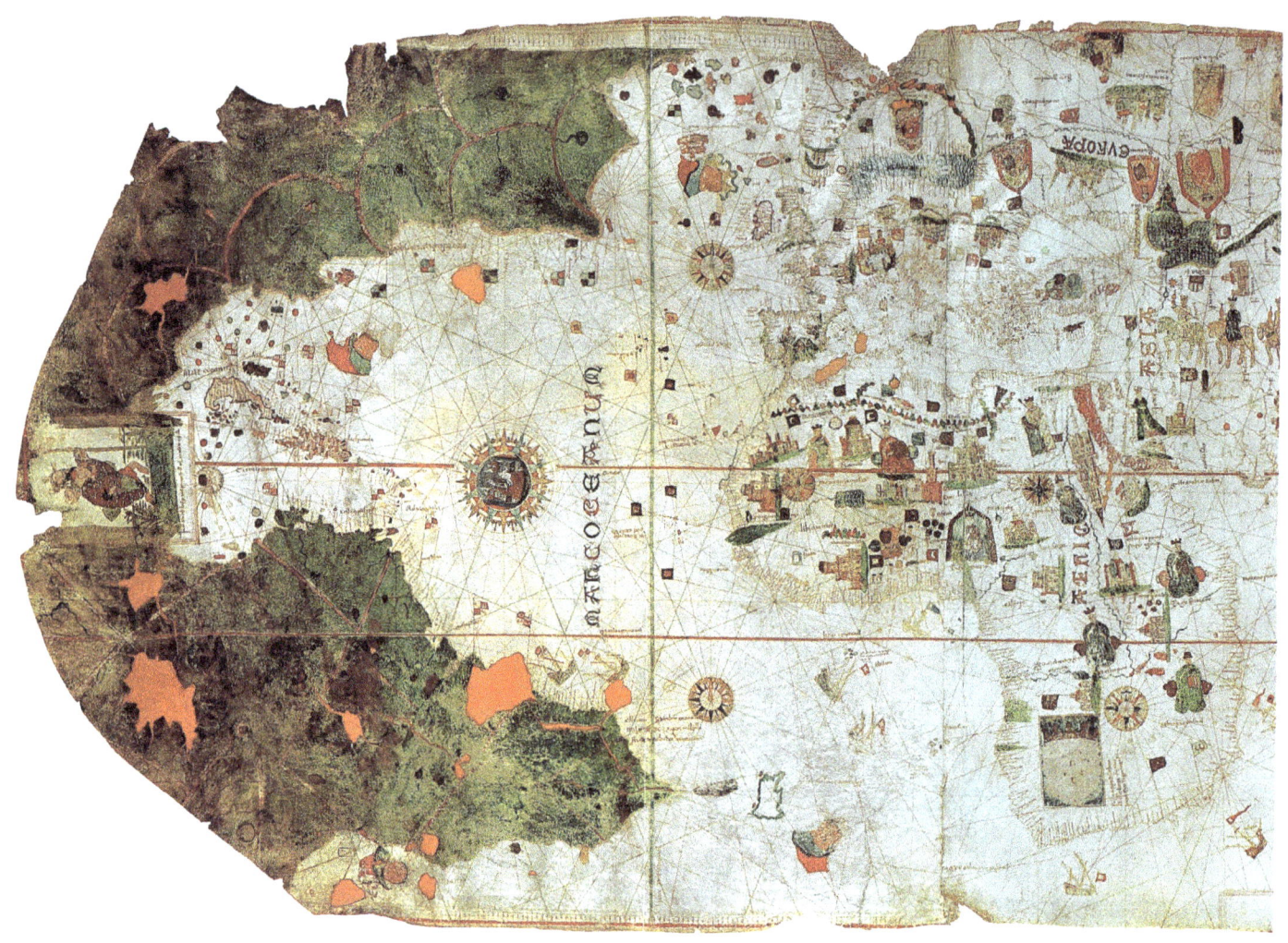

We can picture Henry Hudson, for example, today sailing up the river now named for him, but currently with the magnificent skylines of Manhattan and New Jersey on each side. He would be amazed at the many technological advances that we have come to take for granted. He could now call on data from orbiting space satellites to guide his voyage. He could stay in touch electronically at all times with his homeland, or in fact nearly any other land on Earth.

Probably most astonishing to him would be pictures of the planet Earth from space. He could even zoom in, on command, to specific locations at any time. The beautiful and functional portolani of his day would remain exquisite artefacts, but they would no longer be repositories of the most important information on board his ship. Instead, such maps would be hung on his wall… or included in books such as this.

World Map, 1500.
Juan de la Cosa.
Parchment, 95.5 x 177 cm.
Museo Naval de Madrid,
Madrid. (Map 22)

We have very few writings from the early explorers; the writings that we do have help us imagine a little of their world and times. Before we put the portolani into their historical context, we can first recreate some of the vision

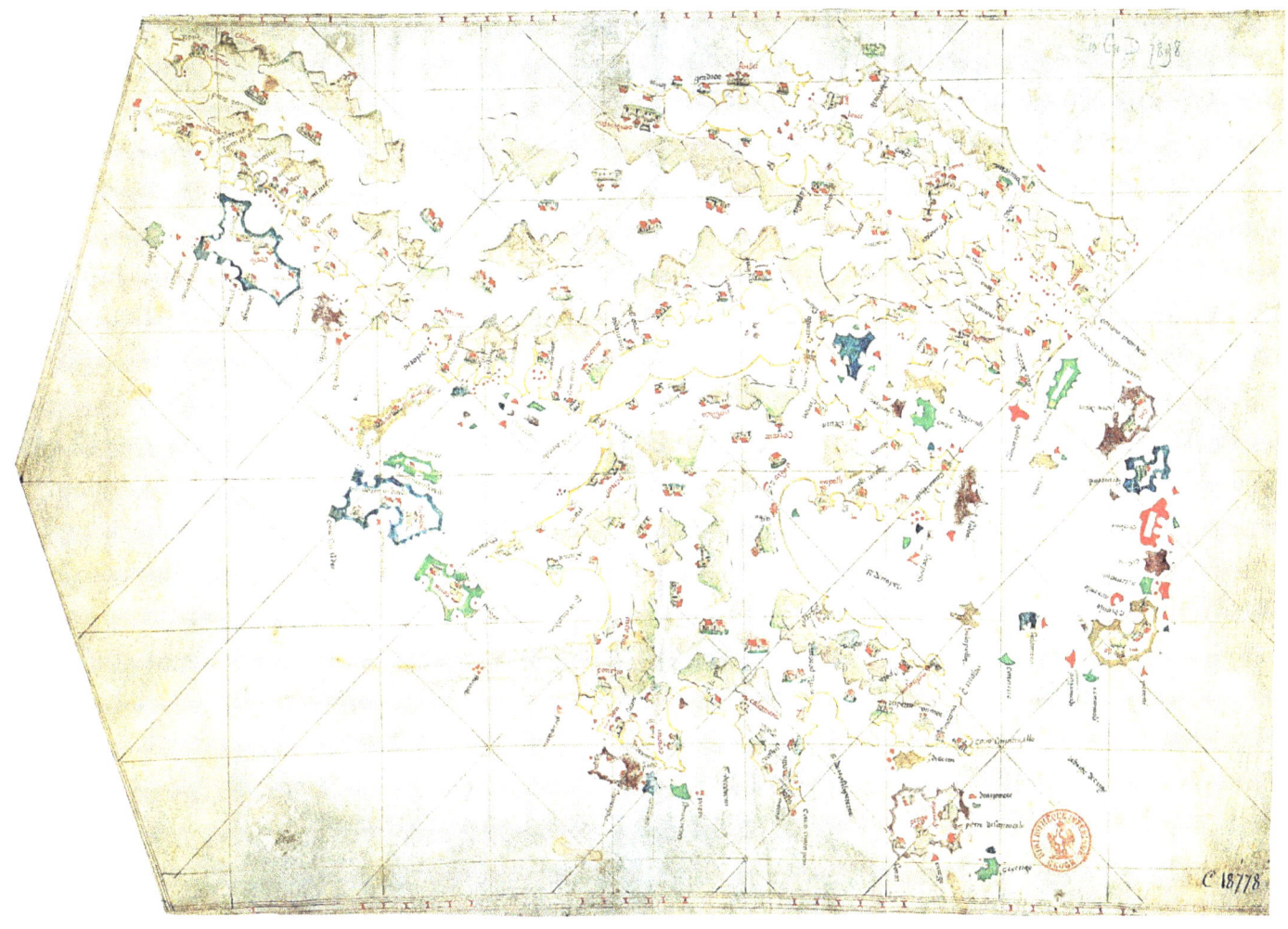

of the pioneers, using their own journals and other writings that have survived the centuries.

Amerigo Vespucci

Nearly 500 years after the earliest Viking sightings of North America, a few weeks before Cabot and about fourteen months before Columbus, Amerigo Vespucci touched down on the mainland of the New World. It was for that reason that the new continent was in 1507 first called 'America' rather than named after Columbus.

The great US writer Ralph Waldo Emerson (1803–1882) mistakenly thought Vespucci named the Western Hemisphere after himself.

Emerson said, 'Amerigo Vespucci, whose highest rank was boatswain's mate in an expedition that never sailed, managed in his lying world to supplant Columbus and baptise half the Earth with his own dishonest name.'

Greek Coasts, 1500 (?).
Unknown artist.
Parchment, 60 x 41 cm.
Bibliothèque nationale
de France, Paris. (Map 23)

But in fact Vespucci referred to the land he had discovered as 'the New World,' not by his own name.

It was a German map-maker Martin Waldseemüller in 1507 who first put the name America on his map, at first only in relation to South America. On that map his marginal note states: 'It is fitting that this fourth part of the world, inasmuch as Americus discovered it, be called *Amerige*, or let us say *Terra Americi*, that is AMERICA.'[11]

It may no longer be shocking for Americans to hear that Columbus was not the first European to reach the New World, but other myths surrounding the early voyages persist even in school textbooks.[12]

With Vespucci we again see the importance of the coastline and surely also of the portolani as well. In a 1597 letter he wrote, 'We sailed with the north-west wind, thus running along the coast with the land ever in sight, continually in our progress observing people along the shore, till after having navigated for two days, we found a place sufficiently secure for the ships. We anchored half a league from land, on which we saw a very great number of people.' He described the skin of the natives as being 'a colour that verges into red like a lion's mane.' But he added, 'I believe that if they went clothed, they would be as white as we are.'[13]

When the Pilgrim Fathers, Puritans all, landed in America, they were surely unaware that the continent was named after an explorer who in 1502 had written a best-selling book that included what some people then and now would call pornography. However, some authorities do suggest that printers might have interpolated such passages into their editions of Vespucci's writing so as to increase sales. Either way, we might wonder how many Europeans came to the New World mainly to find the beautiful and promiscuous natives described in the accounts.[14]

The Cabots

Portrait of John Cabot (Giovanni Caboto), 1455 (?)-1498.

The 'Christopher Columbus' Map, c. 1492. Parchment, 70 x 110 cm. Bibliothèque nationale de France, Paris. (Map 21)

When we think of the Age of Exploration, the names that first come to mind might well be those of the contemporaries Christopher Columbus and Vasco da Gama. However, more than a dozen years before the voyages of these pioneers, John Cabot envisioned and proposed reaching the Far East by sailing west.

Cabot was in the process of obtaining funds for his intended venture when news of the success of Columbus became widespread. Soon, Cabot was among the first explorers from Europe after Columbus to reach the North American coast.

Conversation in the Franciscan Monastery of Santa Maria de La Rabida between the Navigator Christopher Columbus, the Physician Garcia Fernandez, the Priest Juan Perez and Alonzo Pinzón (detail).
Juan Cabral Bejarano.
Oil on canvas.
Monastery of La Rabida, Huelva.

John Cabot (Giovanni Caboto) was born around the middle of the fifteenth century, probably in Genoa. As a young man he traveled the Mediterranean and became a citizen of Venice before moving to England with his sons, of whom Sebastian was to be the most famous.

The lives of John and Sebastian Cabot spanned more than a century of exploration. Their influence on the history of Western civilisation is readily notable if we consider that the property rights in North America to which a European nation was later to lay claim date back not to Columbus but to the landings of John Cabot. At that time he was in the service of King Henry VII of England, who reigned from 1485 to 1509.

In 1497, with at least eighteen men aboard the *Matthew*, he landed on the shores of North America, on the land later to be named Newfoundland. He then may have sailed as far south as the present state of Maine, or as far north as Labrador. That year England claimed what are now Canadian lands for King Henry VII.

Just like Columbus before him, John Cabot returned to Europe with a wealth of new information to contribute to contemporary maps. We now know that much of Cabot's data was incorrect. Like Columbus, he too thought he had reached Asia. We see in the maps influenced by his first voyage that map-makers incorporated some of Cabot's information, but not all.

A year or so after John Cabot's first voyage, he set sail again, this time with five ships. And this time he fully intended sailing beyond his previous landing and, he thought, on to Japan.

One of Cabot's ships returned quickly to England for repairs, while the other four continued on. At least one may have reached the Spanish-held territory in the Caribbean Sea, while another may also have had to return to England. Meanwhile, John Cabot himself was lost at sea.

No contemporary documentation of the second voyage has survived. Yet we shall see that the influence of this voyage is apparent in subsequent maps, including those made by his son, Sebastian.

The discovery in 1497 of mainland North America by John Cabot is well documented. He was a citizen of Venice but was sponsored by England. With our interest here in coastal maps and their role in these discoveries, we note that one letter written in that same year mentions that Cabot was 'very expert in navigation'. Moreover, he 'has the description of the world on a chart, and also on a solid sphere which he has constructed, and on which he shows where he has been; and, proceeding towards the east'.[15]

Christopher Columbus

As a young man Columbus was, among other things, a scholar and seller of maps. Seven years before his most famous 1492 voyage, he read and commented on a book in Latin that related the travels of Marco Polo. Like Fra Mauro, Columbus could hardly be aware of errors in Marco Polo's accounts, including his erroneous location for Japan. Similarly, Columbus had also studied Ptolemy's maps. It had taken twelve centuries for the original Greek version of Ptolemy's work to reach Italy and be translated there, but then it

Portrait of Christopher Columbus, first half of the 16th century. Ridolfo Ghirlandaio (1483-1561). Padiglione del Mare e della Navigazione, Genova.

quickly reached many pre-Renaissance scholars and other intelligent men including Columbus (see p. 59).

However, Columbus had also no idea that Ptolemy had badly underestimated the circumference of the Earth. The miscalculation was soon to cost the lives of many brave sailors who were in inadequate ships and at sea much longer than expected. Above the map-maker's desk the poster should have hung: *Bad maps can cost good lives.*

Armed with such misinformation, Columbus – like John Cabot earlier – fondly imagined that sailing west to India was not only possible, but – and this was crucial – was possible with the quality of the ships available at the time.

Columbus also studied Martin Behaim's globe [Map 20] and Paolo Toscanelli's chart of the world, as described here earlier.

These authoritative resources were included in the presentation by Columbus first to the King of Portugal (who rejected the proposal). He then tried – for seven long years – to make the same proposals to King Ferdinand and Queen Isabella of Spain. He finally got their backing and, as every English-speaking schoolchild learns:

> *Columbus sailed the ocean blue*
> *in fourteen hundred and ninety two.*

Columbus returned to Spain with promises of endless conquests on behalf of the nation. Spain was on its way to building an empire in the Americas and eventually in the Philippines. Maps were vital, and required to be continually updated.

Juan de la Cosa's Map

In 1500, after four Columbus voyages, Juan de la Cosa of Santona drew his now famous map on oxhide [Map 22]. In the nineteenth century the map was discovered in Madrid by Alexander von Humboldt. It was the first of many maps to attempt to show all of Columbus' discoveries. His map takes on special significance since de la Cosa was on the *Santa Maria* with Columbus during the first voyage. Moreover, he was one of the joint-owners of the vessel. (The crew of that pioneering ship surely never imagined that their names and those of all on board the *Niña*, the *Pinta* and the *Santa Maria*, along with maps of their voyages would – 500 years later – be posted on an electronic device for the world to see.)[16]

We would expect all the new information supplied by Columbus to be included on such maps made after his return to Europe. For this reason, what de la Cosa so

Christopher Columbus Presenting the New World Treasures to the Souverains of Spain.
Ricardo Balaca (1844-1880).
Oil on canvas.
Museo Historico Nacional, Buenos Aires.

Planisphere, c. 1505.
Nicolaus de Caverio.
Parchment, 115 x 225 cm.
Bibliothèque nationale de France, Paris. (Map 26)

Compass Dial, 18th century, England.

John Harrison's Marine Chronometer Number 1 (H1), 1730-1735, England. National Maritime Museum, Greenwich.

Octant, c. 1750, England. Mahogany. L'Antiquaire de Marine, Paris.

THE INSTRUMENTS OF NAVIGATION

In the fifteenth century when Prince Henry the Navigator established the first school of nautical education at Sagres, Portugal, even the basic application of the compass to navigation was not yet understood, although it had been invented some 500 years before.

The adaptation by Europeans in around the sixteenth century of the astrolabe to maritime use was a help, but the device had been invented by the Arabs for use on land – it was difficult to use on board ship because of a ship's constant motion.

Even in comparatively recent times, before the invention of speedometers, a navigator would estimate the speed of his ship by throwing overboard a float attached to a long rope, then counting the number of evenly-spaced knots that slipped through his hands during a fixed period of time.

This is the origin of measuring nautical speeds in 'knots'. A knot corresponds to a unit of one nautical mile (in the USA, 6076.1 feet; in Britain, 6,082.7 feet) per hour. For centuries, a 'sand clock' or an hourglass was used for measuring time on board a ship.

The date of the origin of the hourglass is not known, but it was used on board ships in ancient times. We see several listed in the supplies of most expeditions before John Harrison (1693–1776) brought chronometers to ships in the eighteenth century.

The Mariners' Museum has published a study of the evolution of instruments for navigating by celestial bodies, from the ancient *kamál* to the modern-day global positioning systems. This book by Peter Ifland is titled *Taking the Stars: Celestial Navigation from Argonauts to Astronauts*, Krieger Publishing, 1999. It describes the history of sextants and other instruments designed for celestial navigation and includes 'how-to' explanations of the proper use of such instruments.

deliberately left out of his map may be more revealing than what he so carefully put in. It shows the islands of the Caribbean curiously located between two continental coasts, and the coast to the west of the islands – where we might expect to find the most dramatic piece of new information – is actually obscured by a religious icon of St Christopher – not coincidentally the patron saint of Columbus. (Even then the use St Christopher images connected with transportation was widely practised. The tradition was that 'once upon a time' a man, later appropriately named Christopher or 'Christ-bearer', carried the boy Jesus across treacherous waters.)

The apparent idiosyncrasy in that de la Cosa map is explained as we learn that Columbus had demanded that Juan sign an affidavit that stated that Cuba was not an island but was part of (what he thought was) Asia's mainland.[17]

Here and elsewhere we see that some explorers, map-makers and their sponsors were at times nothing more or less than greedy entrepreneurs even if often also truth-seeking historians and scientists. Also, some – including Columbus – typically spoke highly of religious values even while they planned and practised slavery, torture, and even worse.

Near the end of his return voyage to Europe from North America, Christopher Columbus wrote to the treasurer of Aragon who had helped to put together the finance for Columbus' expedition.

Columbus stated, 'I write this to tell you how in thirty-three days I sailed to the Indies with the fleet that the illustrious King and Queen, our Sovereigns, gave me, where I discovered a great many islands, inhabited by numberless people … When I came to Juana, I followed the coast of that isle toward the west, and found it so extensive that I thought it might be the mainland, the province of Cathay; and as I found no towns nor villages on the sea-coast … I continued the said route … I sailed one hundred and seven leagues along the sea-coast of Juana, in a straight line from west to east. I can therefore assert that this island is larger than England and Scotland together, since beyond these one hundred and seven leagues there remained at the west point two provinces where I did not go, one of which they call Avan, the home of men with tails.'[18]

The story of Columbus is best told interwoven as it was in actual events with the lives of the three Pinzón brothers. Together they have a unique page in the history of navigation.

Francisco Martín and Vicente Yáñez not only became sailors, as did their older brother Martín Alonso before them, but all three were with Columbus on his first transatlantic voyage. Martín was in fact probably one of the owners of the *Pinta* and the *Niña*.

Cantino's Planisphere, 1502.
Three parchment sheets,
220 x 105 cm.
Biblioteca Estense, Modena.
(Map 25)

While Columbus captained the *Santa Maria*, Martín Pinzón captained the *Pinta*, on which Francisco served. Vicente, the youngest Pinzón brother, captained the *Niña* and would on subsequent voyages become a renowned explorer. He explored much of the east coasts of Central and South America – and by doing so he eventually undermined Columbus' claim to have reached the Indies. Before the discoveries of Vicente's voyages were generally acknowledged, however, Columbus died claiming and apparently believing that he had reached not only islands off the coast of Asia, but Asia itself during his four voyages.

The cartographer Juan de Solfs accompanied Vicente on an expedition in 1506, during which a careful survey of the Yucatán peninsula was made and an excellent natural harbor discovered in what is now Honduras. It would be settled and become today's port of Trujillo. Meanwhile Juan de Solfs returned home, and subsequent portolani incorporated data from his detailed survey.

Even though Vicente was later to be appointed Governor of Puerto Rico, his achievements were destined to remain less prominent in the wake of the fame of Columbus.

Near the end of the famous 1492 voyage of the three ships of Columbus, after seeing flights of birds headed south-west, Martín argued with Columbus that the fleet should turn further south where he calculated Zipangri, or Cathay, would be. Columbus, however, altered only to the south-west. A few hours after the argument with Columbus, a crewman on Martín's *Niña* was the first to sight land.

As when considering every notable point in history, we can ask ourselves what might have happened if other choices had been made. Had Columbus not altered his course, the fleet most likely would have sailed towards and landed on the Florida coast. 'He would have reached the sand and marsh of the Florida coast, near Cape Canaveral,' according to some scholars.

The exact location of Columbus's first landfall is not known, but several experts identify it as the island later named San Salvador by the Spaniards.

The Pinzón

Of the Pinzón brothers, it was to be Martín who would draw the most attention of historians, but not primarily because of his navigational skills. Rather, he is much better known for deserting Columbus for about six weeks once the expedition reached Cuba. Seeking personal fortune, the impatient Martín ventured out on his own in search of an island described to him by the

Departure of the Santa Maria, the Pinta and the Niña from Palos in 1492. Antonio Cabral Bejarano (1788-1861).
Oil on canvas.
Monastery of La Rabida, Huelva.

natives as being rich with gold. He never found that island – but he did discover Hispaniola before Columbus.

By his own records, even without first doing any reconnaissance, Columbus claimed possession of the land that he had reached for Spain in the name of Ferdinand and Isabella. The legendary scene of Columbus holding the flag of Spain as he claimed the territory on behalf of his sponsors is often imagined by painters. However, such scenes prompt one of the most intriguing unanswered questions of all in the history of exploration. Where did Columbus really think he was?[19]

It is not likely that Columbus would claim to take possession of a territory of the Great Khan; Spain was not seeking to invade Asia. Moreover, after seeing this land and its natives on many occasions over the next twelve years, Columbus surely noted little resemblance of this land to the places and people described by Marco Polo. Yet he always later claimed that he really had reached Cathay, the Indies, or at least islands near by.

Of course, how could he say otherwise and still obtain financing for subsequent voyages? Moreover, he was ambitious and coveted the highest naval title. He also yearned to be put in charge of a force of 110,000 men so as to 'go and take possession of the Holy Places' on another Crusade to the Holy Land. Profits from his plundering would finance this venture.[20]

Rejoining Columbus after his unsuccessful venture on his own, Martín Pinzón was apparently forgiven. But he betrayed his colleagues once more, breaking with them and then trying to return to Spain independently, apparently in order to claim the glory of the discoveries before Columbus could.

Nature did not cooperate in this scheme, however, for stormy winds kept Martín with the *Pinta* from reaching Europe before Columbus and the *Niña*. (The *Santa Maria* was wrecked before the two surviving ships returned. In spite of many 'replicas' and drawings, little is known of the actual appearance of the *Santa Maria*.)

Martín died soon after returning to the Andalusian port of Palos, the Pinzóns' home town and the port from which Columbus first sailed to the New World. Ten years after Martín's death, Vicente captained a fleet across the Atlantic once again.

In 1500 he reached Brazil. However, he may not have been the first to do so. Historians generally build an impressive case for Pedro Cabral's being the first. Some evidence also points to Amerigo Vespucci as having that distinction. It is unlikely that we will ever know.

Portolano of Dijon, c. 1510.
Unknown artist.
Parchment (in irregular triangular format), max. dimensions 99.5 x 66.5 cm.
Bibliothèque municipale, Dijon. (Map 27)

Atlantic Ocean, 1513.
Piri Re'is.
Parchment, 90 x 65 cm.
Topkapi Sarayi Museum, Istanbul. (Map 28)

The Miller Atlas (The Azores), c. 1519.
Lopo Homem and others.
Parchment, 41.5 x 59 cm.
Bibliothèque nationale de France, Paris. (Map 29)

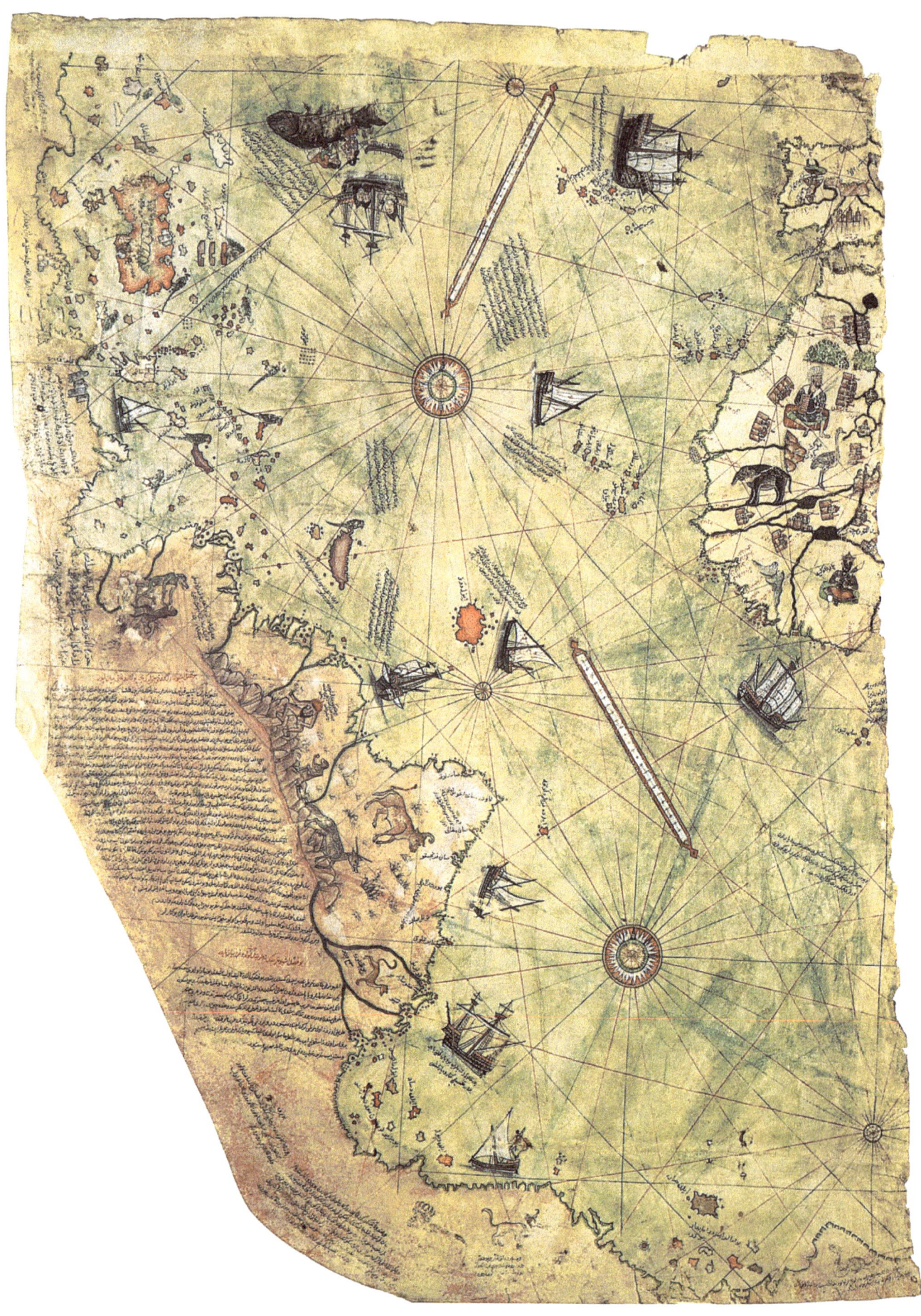

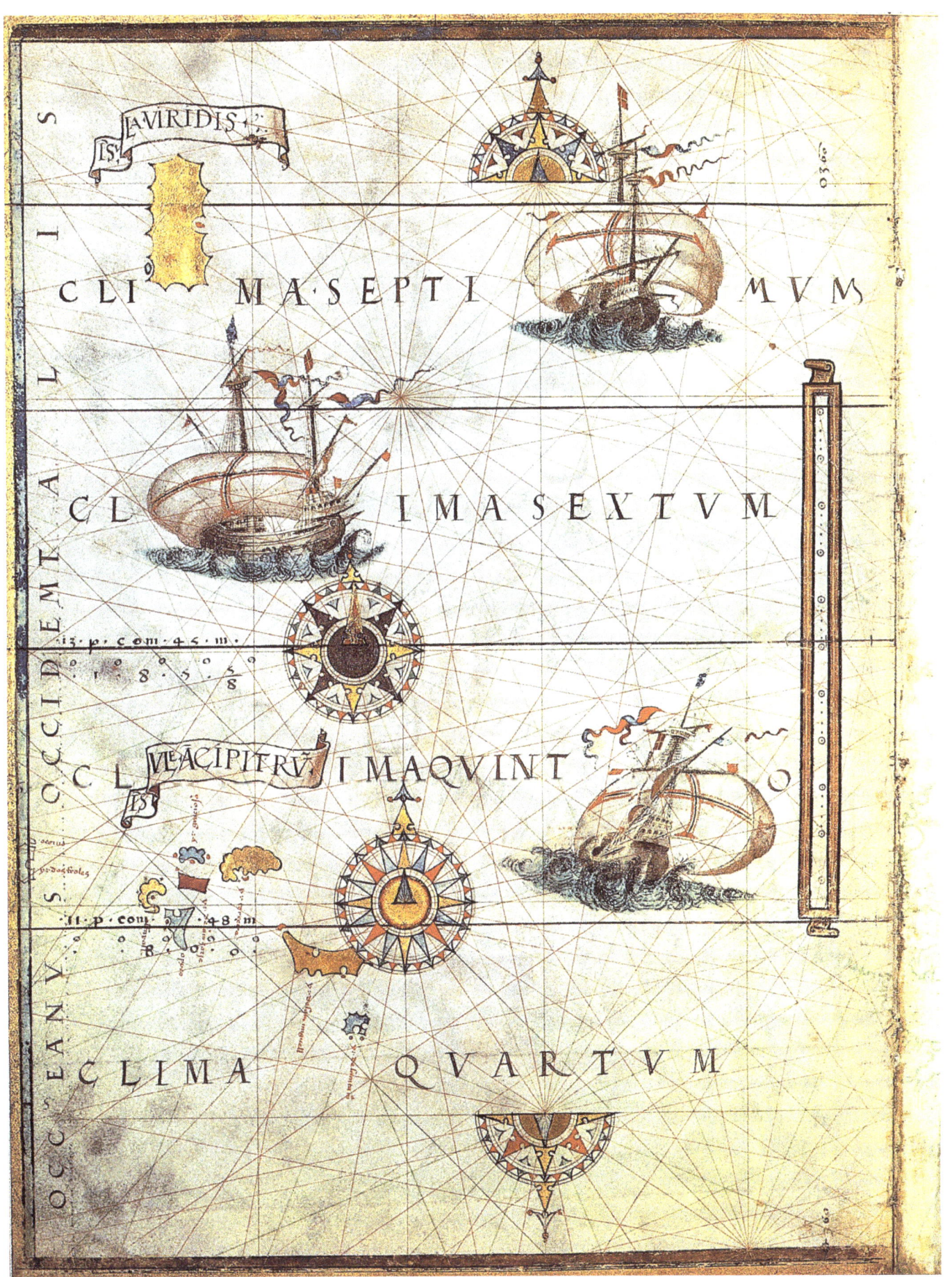

Vicente sailed up the coast of South America to the Caribbean Sea and to Hispaniola. Along the way, he captured natives and attempted to force information from them about the land's resources. Because of such un-thinking cruelty – and because of the invasion of their land in general by Europeans – these explorers have obviously never been particularly admired by the indigenous people of the Americas or by others aware of the injustices imposed on the native inhabitants then and since.

Martín Pinzón and Columbus were the first European slave traders in the Americas. On his first voyage, Columbus brought ten natives he'd had abducted back to Spain, putting them on display – along with American parrots – and parading them through the streets for the amusement of Spaniards.[21]

Even the clergy at that time did not acknowledge the immorality of slavery. 'King Ferdinand had sent a gift to Pope Innocent VIII of one hundred Moorish slaves, which the Pope shared with the cardinal and close friends.'[22]

Illustration from the *Voyage de Gouin de Beauchesne*, 1698-1701.
Jacques Gouin de Beauchesne (1652-1730).
Watercolour on paper.
Service historique de la Marine, Vincennes.

Juan Ponce de León

Columbus's second expedition to the New World included a young crewmember named Juan Ponce de León. As a teenager he had joined his country's fight against the Moors of Granada. After helping to suppress native revolts on Hispaniola,

he was given his government's permission to take over the governorship of Puerto Rico. As further Spanish acknowledgement of his success, he was allowed to settle 'the island of Bimini'. A famous legend holds that Ponce de León was desperate to find the source of a rejuvenating tonic, the 'Fountain of Youth', described to him by Caribbean natives. Of course he never found anything of the sort – but he did discover Florida.

With three ships Ponce de León sailed north, through the Bahamas into the Atlantic, then west to a desolate beach a few miles north of modern St Augustine. And so he became the first Spaniard to set foot on the continent to be called North America.

Hugging the coastline his ships then sailed south and rounded the tip of the 'continent'. Sailing north again and tracing the west coast, he discovered that the land was a peninsula. He named it 'the land of the flowers', apparently not for the literal appropriateness but in honor of Easter Sunday (Pascua Florida or 'Easter of the flowers').

After returning to Spain, Ponce de León was knighted and received a royal commission to colonise Florida, but he didn't return to the peninsula for seven years. When he finally did return, unlike other invaders – especially most of those from Spain – he did not mistreat the natives. Nonetheless, in 1521 he was killed, ironically, by a native.

Illustration from the *Voyage de Gouin de Beauchesne*, 1698-1701.
Jacques Gouin de Beauchesne (1652-1730).
Watercolour on paper.
Service historique de la Marine, Vincennes.

Bartolomé de Las Casas

Diseases were unintentionally exchanged between the European invaders and the natives of the Americas. That was inevitable and may have even had some biological advantages in the long run, such as when 'hybrid vigor' results from interracial breeding. But there was also deliberate genocide, as well as slavery and other barbaric acts by European invaders, especially against the amazingly sophisticated cultures of the Aztec and Inca civilisations. In the Caribbean, for example, the native population was all but exterminated.

The brutality in the Americas of the Europeans, especially of the Spanish, had its critics even at the very time of the invasions. The most notable of these critics was Bartolomé de Las Casas, who in 1540 presented to the Emperor Charles V the results of his investigative reporting titled *A Brief Account of the Destruction of the Indies*.

The military leaders that conquered the people and lands of the New World during the sixteenth century were known as *conquistadores*. Hernán Cortés conquered Mexico; Francisco Pizarro conquered Peru.

De Las Casas reported what many others knew but ignored or in some cases even encouraged: the conquistadors were allowed to enslave, torture, or demand tribute from the natives in whatever way they wished. It was not exceptional for invaders to dismember, enslave or otherwise maltreat the natives if they were unable to pay taxes or if they did not bend to the invader's demands. Often the same soldiers who inflicted such punishments were simultaneously very conscientious about their religious practices.

Some Church officials were co-conspirators in the exploitative practices. Many others at least knew all about the persecution of the natives at the hands of the conquistadors.

The Catholic Church certainly knew of the inhumane practices of the Inquisition as applied in the New World. A museum corresponding to one such original site of torture exists even today in Colombia as a painful reminder of the tragic truth about which de Las Casas wrote.

One of the most articulate essays against the Inquisition in the eighteenth century was by Louis chevalier de Jaucourt (1704–1779) in Denis Diderot's *Encyclopaedia*. His article on anti-slavery is equally strong.

However, Pope Clement XIII condemned the *Encyclopaedia* as 'containing false, pernicious, and scandalous doctrines and propositions, inducing unbelief and scorn for religion.' Articles on 'priests' and 'theocracy' were very critical of the papacy.

The Miller Atlas (Madagascar),
c. 1519.
Lopo Homem and others.
Parchment, 41.5 x 59 cm.
Bibliothèque nationale
de France, Paris. (Map 30)

Bartolomé de Las Casas (detail).
Oil on canvas.
Archivo General de Indias,
Seville.

Illustration from *Journal of Discovery of the Sources of the Nile*, 1863.
John Hanning Speke
(1827-1864).
Private collection.

The Last Mile of Livingstone,
in *The Life and Explorations of Dr David Livingstone*,
1878.
David Livingstone
(1813-1873).

SLAVES

The abducting, selling and buying of humans was legal in many countries over a good number of centuries. However immoral, most European countries and many individuals sought profit and power by means of the slave trade.

Shortly before the time of Columbus, a Venetian merchant (possibly a former nobleman) Alvise da Cadamosto (c. 1432–c.1480) was a slave trader for the Portuguese. He sailed between Lisbon and ports along the north-west coast of Africa. So did Diogo Gomes (c. 1440–c. 1482), who followed in da Cadamosto's wake but pushed further south into the rich West African slave-trading area of the Guinea Coast.

As a governor in the New World, Columbus set up a system of taxation that was later described by his own son, Ferdinand. 'Whenever an Indian delivered his tribute, he was to receive a brass or copper token which he must wear about his neck as proof that he had made his payment. Any Indian found without such a token was punished.' According to James Loewen, the punishment – which Columbus' son chose not to mention – was the amputation of the Indian's hands.

Meanwhile, in South America, Alonso de Ojeda (1477–1515), a captain on the second voyage of Columbus, enslaved an Indian village along the Colombian coast. He eventually failed to establish a colony there, but his violence fuelled the antagonism of the natives and contributed to their continual attacks on the invading Spanish.

At the start of the sixteenth century, in Puerto Real, the first European settlement in the New World founded by Columbus near La Navidad, the Spanish also enslaved local natives, euphemistically calling them 'Indio de Servicio'. Conquering Europeans were at no loss for other such rationalisations for slavery even though many of them professed to be Christians.

In 1542, Spain banned enslaving Caribbean Indians. Pope Paul III had done likewise in 1537. Nonetheless, priests continued to accompany some of the slave-trading voyages, such as the one in 1567, from Lima, under Alvaro de Mendaña de Neyra. Some might argue that the Church – at least by not speaking out against these atrocities – was a co-conspirator in the slave trade and land-grab activities of the conquistadors.

In Peru, the Spanish conquistadors forced natives to labor in the mines, while in the Caribbean, African slaves were imported to work on the plantations. In the 1650s, in the Spanish colonies of the Americas the Portuguese were the main purveyors of African slaves, bringing them from their trading settlements on the West African coast.

Less surprising was the cruel slave trading of privateers and pirates, such as John Hawkins, who commanded slave-trading expeditions to Africa and the Caribbean. Francis Drake accompanied him on a few such slave-trade voyages in 1566 and 1567. Drake was knighted in 1581. Martin Frobisher's early voyages were also slaving expeditions. He too was rewarded with a royal commission in 1571.

The report on Spanish brutality in the New World sent to Charles V in 1540 by Bartolomé de Las Casas brought slavery to the attention of many Europeans, but the exploitation of humans still went on for centuries.

One of the principal collaborators with Denis Diderot on the *Encyclopaedia*, de Jaucourt, spoke out against slavery in that major work of the Enlightenment. However, the work as a whole was condemned by Pope Clement XIII, as noted here concerning de Jaucourt's article on 'the Inquisition'. The work reached fewer influential people than it should have at the time because excommunication was threatened for those who even possessed, let alone read, the *Encyclopaedia*.

During its first century, the United States was certainly not the first country to condone slavery, even if it was to be among the last to abolish it. Most of its founding fathers were slave-owners, even as they wrote and spoke eloquently against such a concept, or 'certain inalienable rights' of all humans.

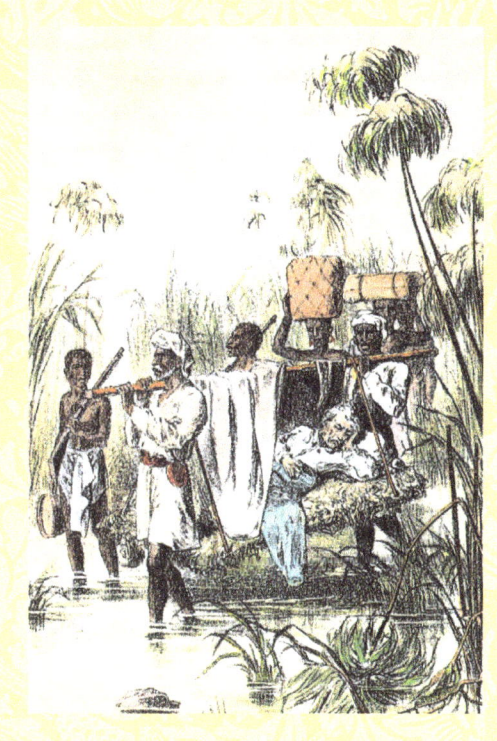

It is well known that slavery was embedded in every aspect of life in the South of the United States, but from the colonial era to the Civil War it was also an important part of the North as well. In 1750, slaves represented more than 10 percent of New York City's population. From 1792 to 1800, more than 400 of the 600 workers who helped erect the White House and the US Capitol were black slaves. The plantation owner appropriated their wages of $5 a month.

In the 1700s and early 1800s, newspapers in the United States accepted advertising for businesses involved with slave trading. The nation's oldest continuously published newspaper, *The Courant* in Hartford, Connecticut, founded in 1764, ran slave-era ads from 1764 to 1823. Centuries later, in July 2000, it formally apologised for doing so. *The Courant* and many other papers ran advertisements for the sale of slaves as well as for rewards for the return of runaways. Even the *Pennsylvania Gazette* accepted slave advertisements, although its founder, Benjamin Franklin, did not approve of slavery itself. At the time of writing, not all of the other newspapers that still exist, and that published such advertising before slavery was abolished by Abraham Lincoln in 1848, have apologised.

Slaves were exported primarily from Africa to America and Europe in ships designed or adapted especially for their human cargoes. A less familiar trade route was by the British to Spanish America.

A serious investigation of how the slave-ship revolts, especially those on the *Amistad*, are depicted in fiction is made by Maggie Montesiones Sale in *The Slumbering Volcano*. Concerning the *Amistad* in particular, see Mary Cable's *Black Odyssey*.

But the pope was referring to the work in general, condemning it all because of those anti-Catholic articles.

Pánfilo de Narváez

In Hispaniola only six years after Columbus, Pánfilo de Narváez was assigned to head up an expeditionary force that made a seven-year survey of Cuba during which he successfully mapped the entire island. He was later sent by the governor to take over an expedition under the command of Hernán Cortés, but he was instead ambushed, defeated and imprisoned for two years.

He returned to Spain but received yet another commission to sail back to the New World, which he did with six ships and 500 men. Once in Cuba, 140 of his men deserted. De Narváez continued on to Florida but eventually lost his entire expedition. He and his small crew died at sea after a storm near the mouth of the Mississippi. In Spain it was presumed the expedition was entirely lost, but some had survived and continued west by land.

The de Las Casas report especially stressed the cruelty of Narváez for it was estimated that he had massacred thousands of natives.

Bartolomeu Dias

Near the end of the fifteenth century, gaining access to India's commerce was the most important goal for Portugal; that trade was vital to its commercial survival. It commissioned expeditions to India by sea as well as by land. Reports about the lucrative markets from the successful overland venture through Egypt certainly influenced the country's sponsorship of Columbus' first voyage. But earlier, in 1487, the Portuguese navigator Bartolomeu Dias was given a fleet of three ships and the assignment to find the southernmost point of Africa (see above).

Dias was also commanded to find Prester John, the mythical king of a large part of western Africa. He didn't find the king, but in 1489 he did become the first European to successfully sail past the Cape of Good Hope.

The Miller Atlas (Arabia and India), c. 1519. Lopo Homem and others. Parchment, 41.5 x 59 cm. Bibliothèque nationale de France, Paris. (Map 31)

Portrait of Bartolomeu Dias. Oil on canvas. Museo Marinha, Lisbon.

Vasco da Gama

Vasco da Gama may have been only twenty-one when Columbus returned for the first time from the New World to Spain, but he was far from inexperienced. As an even younger man he had fought against Castile, helping to seize French ships.

He had already learned navigation, mathematics, and astronomy. He had also seen at first hand how to manage many people and large projects as his father, the civil governor of Sines, did in their home town in southern Portugal. He matured into the greatest of his country's explorers.

Portugal then and now has Lisbon, one of the best harbors in all of Europe. Its nearest national neighbor, Spain, was also its great rival regarding exploration. On its eastern border, Spain formed a barrier between Portugal and the rest of Europe; Portugal's west coast ironically opened the way to the east and thereby to its economic survival.

Towards that goal, Portugal gradually developed control of the commercial trade between Europe and the major ports of West Africa. As intense business competition created an atmosphere that threatened to break out into war with Spain, Portugal even built forts at strategic locations on the Guinea Coast to protects its maritime traffic.

However, anticipating the danger of such a war between the 'superpowers' of their day, the Pope (who clearly favored Spain) drew a political north-south line in the ocean, granting Spain the right to trade west of that line. The Vatican had a direct influence on issues of commerce, especially in countries where Catholicism was the dominant religion, including Spain and Portugal at that time.

As so often happens when Church and state are not clearly distinct, heated controversy, compromise and even war resulted. In this historic case, the eventual settlement was the 1494 Treaty of Tondesillas. It created a dividing line similar to the Pope's solution, but this time Portugal benefited most because the line was drawn about a thousand miles further west.

Now a section of what would later be named Brazil was on Portugal's side. However, Portugal's first interest was not the vague visions of treasure in the New World to the west, but the very tangible wealth of India to the east.

In this volatile political environment, da Gama studied the voyages of his predecessors, surely using whatever portolani were available to him. His challenge was to find a voyage around Africa, across the Indian Ocean to India itself. He was put in charge of four vessels and 170 seamen. The ships were stocked with a three-year supply of rations and valuable trade goods, as well as trinkets that he hoped to trade for spices and gold.

Vasco's brother Paolo was in command of one of the ships. Unfortunately, Paolo would not be one of the fifty-four survivors of the expedition. Due to his diminished crew, da Gama was forced to abandon two of the ships during the

The Miller Atlas (Malaysia, Sumatra), c. 1519. Lopo Homem and others. Parchment, 41.5 x 59 cm. Bibliothèque nationale de France, Paris. (Map 32)

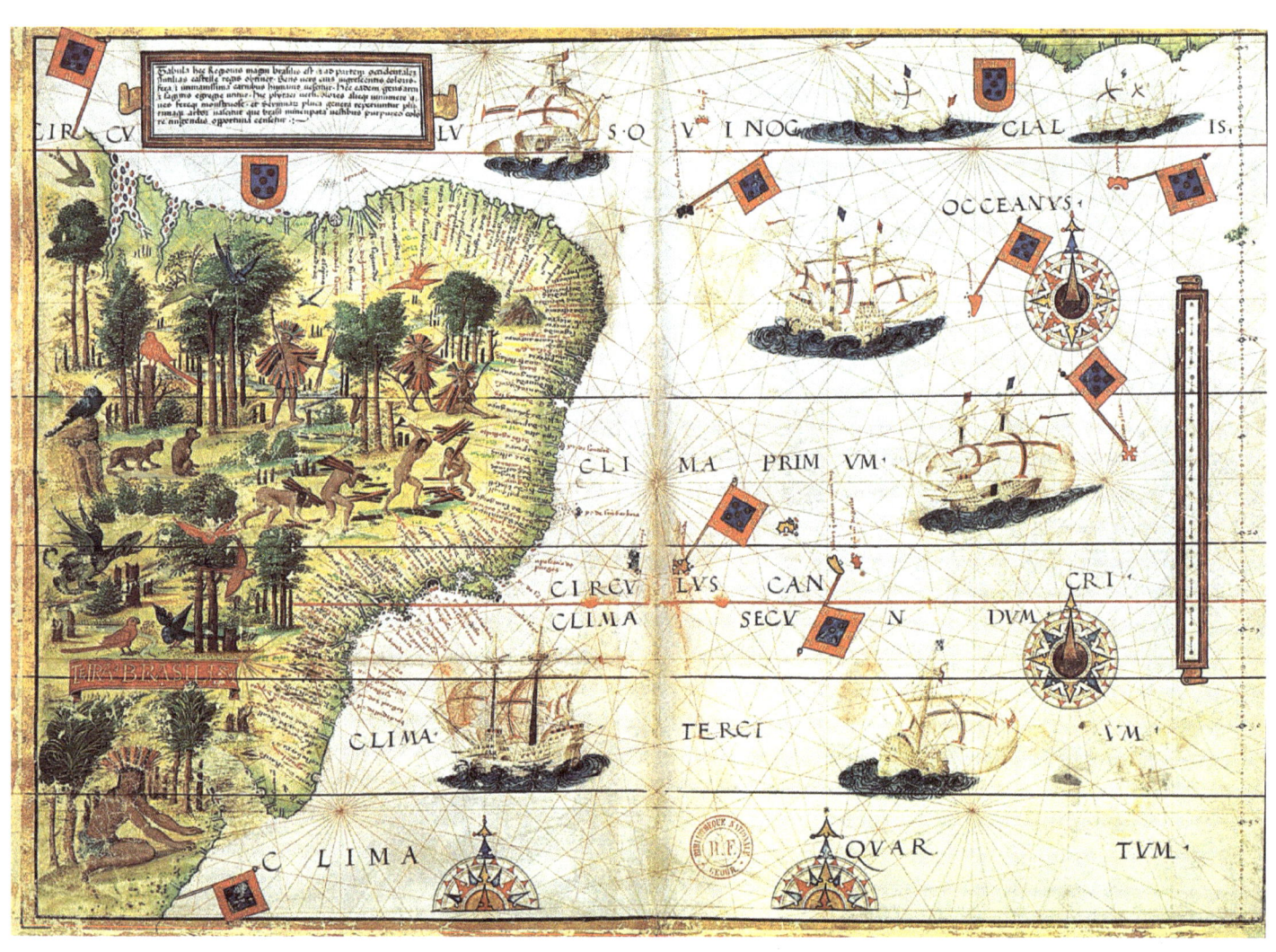

return leg of the torturous 27,000-mile journey. The Indian Ocean accounted for about 2,300 miles each way of the expedition.

Sailing West to go East

Unlike previous navigators, da Gama did not keep his southbound fleet close to the coastline of West Africa. On the contrary, in 1497 he was the first to swing far to the west so as to take advantage of the wind currents, completing the south-eastern journey in a remarkably accurate voyage to the southern tip of Africa in about eight months out of Lisbon. In 1500 Pedro Alvares Cabral, a friend of da Gama, would swing even further west in his voyage to India.

Da Gama ran into hostile local rulers during his visits to ports up the East African coast. However, the Sultan of Malindi provided him with the help of a native navigator. His fleet then crossed the Indian Ocean in twenty-three days. The guide, however, deserted the project in Calcutta.

Without expert assistance and because of stormy winds the fleet took three months on a difficult return trip. During the voyage back down the East African coast, food and water was supplied again by the Sultan of Malindi to help fight the scurvy and other diseases that had devastated the crew.

Da Gama returned with only a few spices, but the discovery of a maritime route to India from Europe was a triumph. Immediately, Portugal began dominating seaborne commerce with India and then the Spice Islands. The Portuguese at first thought the Hindus they encountered were Christians.

Meanwhile, the Arabs correctly saw the Portuguese as a threat to their commercial trade with India. Moreover, the trinkets the Portuguese brought with them turned out to be more appropriate for Africans than for Indians. Consequently, da Gama was unable to complete any genuine commercial agreements between Portugal and India.

PORTOLANI DURING THIS PERIOD

Portolani [such as Maps 11–16] from the early part of the fifteenth century might well have been available to the older Pinzón, Cabot, Columbus, Vespucci and explorers after them. For del Canto, the younger Pinzón, Vasco de Gama, Ponce de León and subsequent navigators, many improved maps (such as Maps 17–19) may have been available. The explorers active after the second half of the fifteenth century would have seen maps (similar to Map/globe 20 and Map 21) with even more detail.

The Miller Atlas (Brazil),
c. 1519.
Lopo Homem and others.
Parchment, 41.5 x 59 cm.
Bibliothèque nationale
de France, Paris. (Map 33)

The Miller Atlas (Atlantic),
c. 1519.
Lopo Homem and others.
Parchment, 61 x 118 cm.
Bibliothèque nationale
de France, Paris. (Map 34)

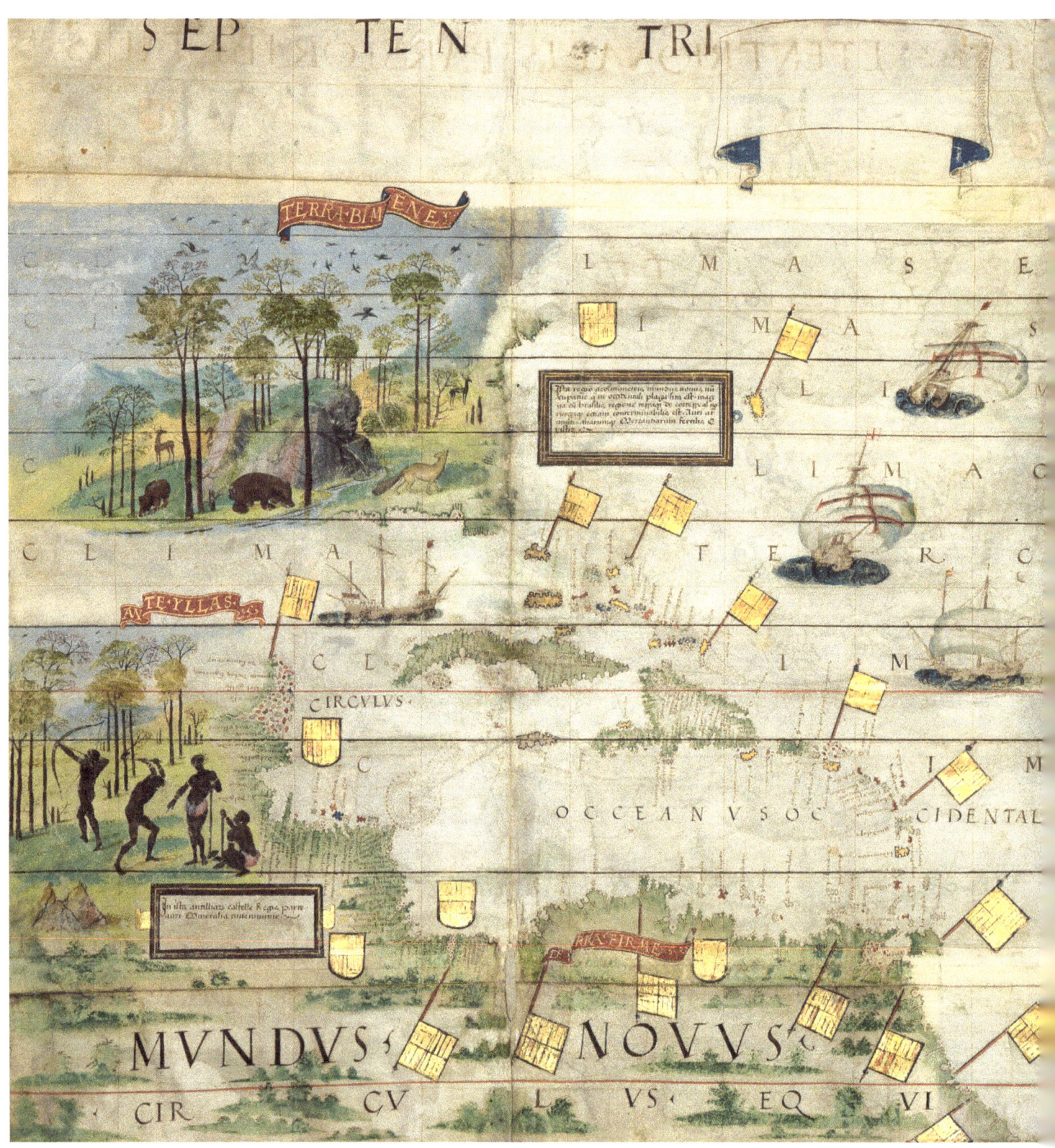

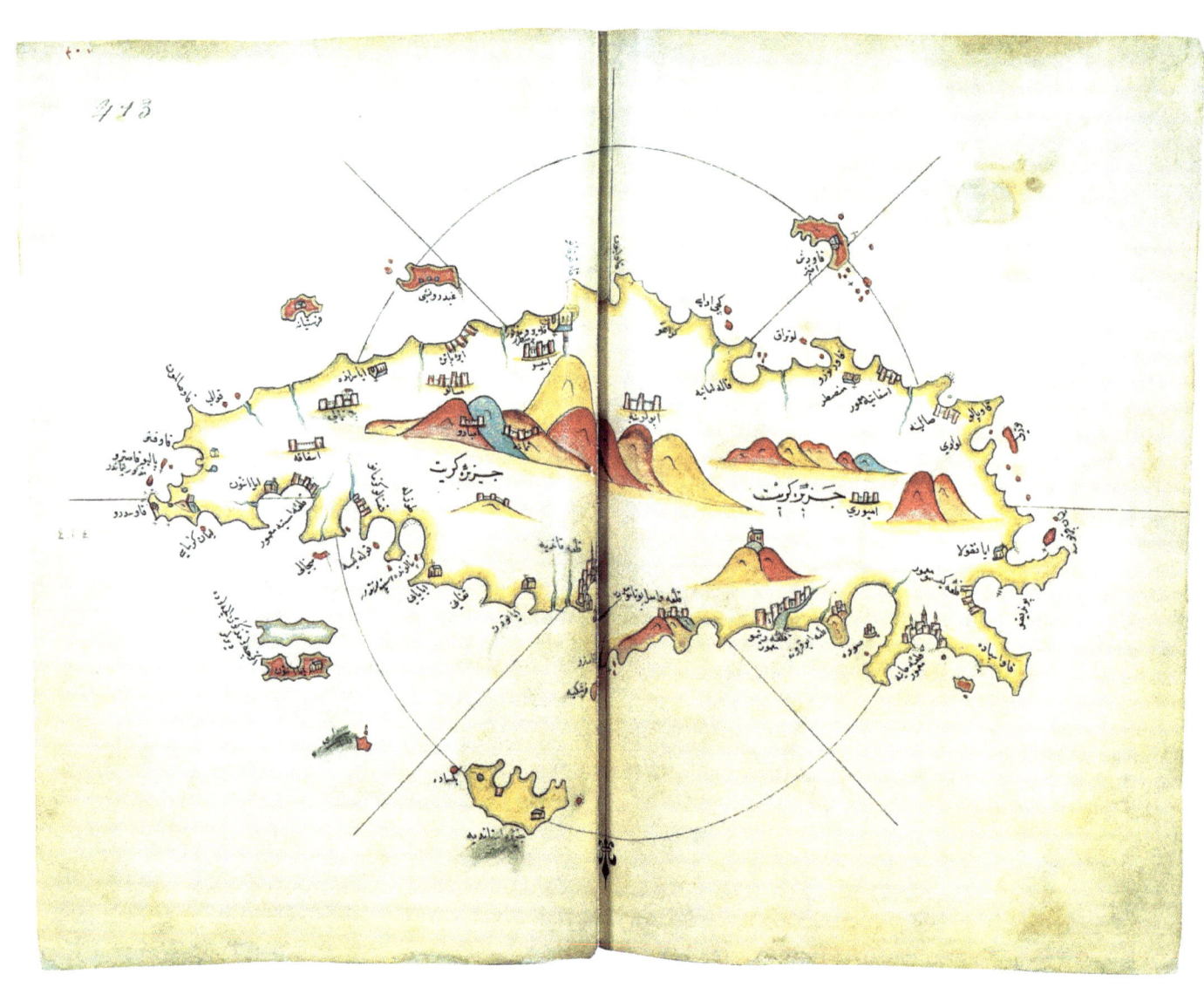

Kitab-i-Bahriye
('The Book of the Seafarers') (Crete), 1525-1526.
Piri Re'is.
Parchment, 35 x 46 cm.
Bibliothèque nationale de France, Paris.
(Map 36)

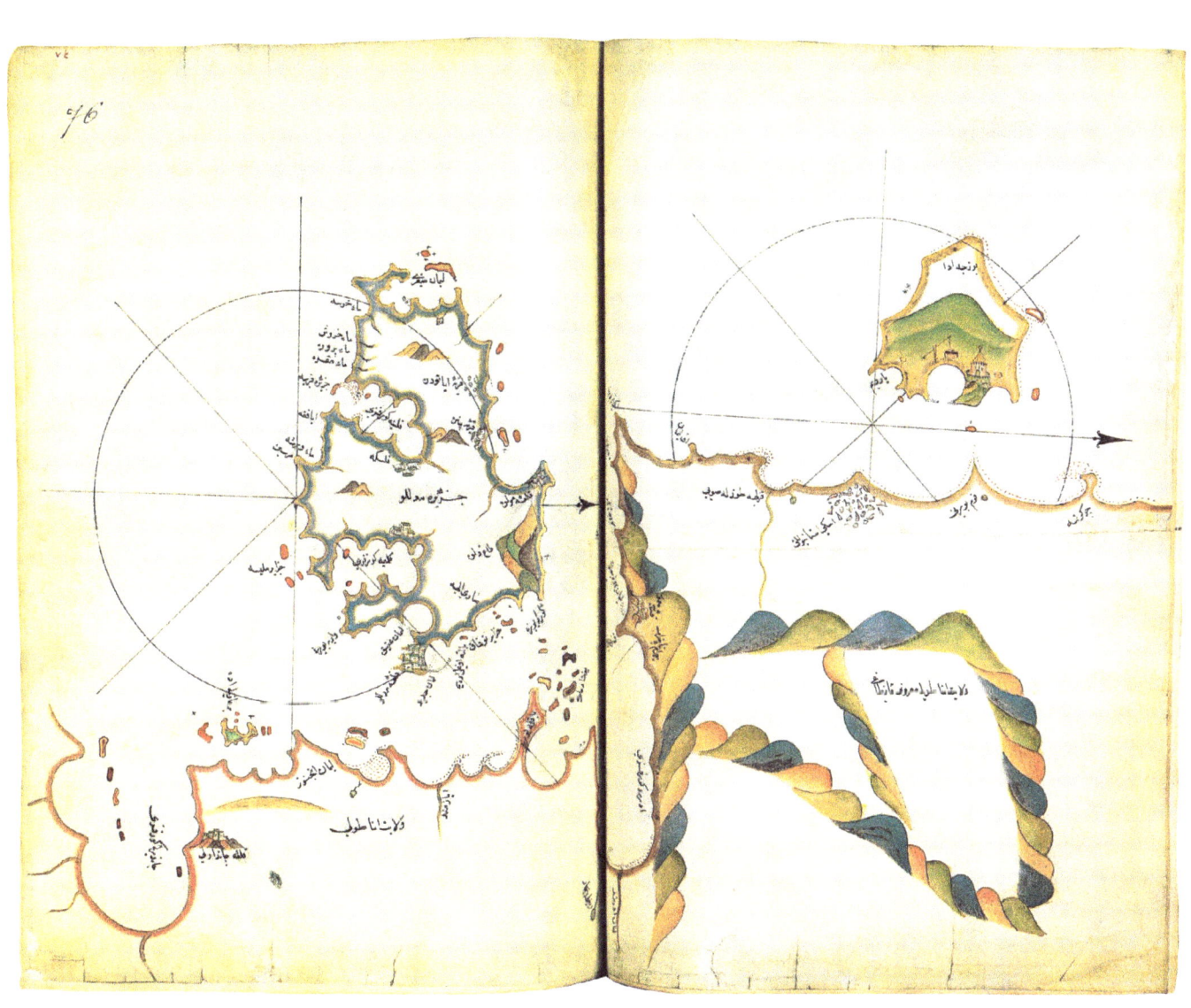

Kitab-i-Bahriye
(*'The Book of the Seafarers'*)
(*Coast of Asia Minor*), 1525-1526.
Piri Re'is.
Parchment, 35 x 46 cm.
Bibliothèque nationale de France, Paris.
(Map 35)

The famous maps of Columbus [Map 21] and of Juan de la Cosa [Map 22] are mentioned in the text above.

Independent Portolani

Maps 13 and 14, dated 1420, stand out from preceding schools. These maps were included in a best-selling book by Cristoforo Buondelmonte that was translated into Greek and Latin. The book with its maps introduced a new approach to marine cartography that was followed until the seventeenth century.

Map 16 is extremely rare, a real Catalan navigation map. While there is no interior nomenclature, descriptions of the Black and Mediterranean Seas are visible. Proportions within the whole basin are more exact than in previous maps. Map 17, a detail from a much larger map, has similar details and views of the most important cities.

It also attempts to achieve the right proportions between the Atlantic and Mediterranean. Representation of the British Isles is greatly improved over that of previous maps, especially of the east coast and Ireland. The artist, Petrus Roselli, is one of the most important cartographers of the fifteenth century. This is one of only six known maps drawn up by him during his most productive period, 1447–1468.

The oldest known globe, made in 1492 under the direction of Martin Behaim, actually comprises pieces of parchment stuck onto a wooden sphere. Map 20 is a copy dating from 1847.

The Dutch School

Maps 70, 79, 87, and 88 are of the Dutch school, centered in Amsterdam (1450–1548). They show the important influence of the English school at Bristol circa 1400. They themselves influenced the school at La Rochelle (1483–1559).

La Baie de la Table in *Description de l'Afrique*, 1686.
Olfert Dapper (1639-1689).
Bibliothèque nationale de France, Paris.

The brothers Harmen and Marten Jansz made copies of maps, such as their very practical map of the Atlantic Ocean, the Mediterranean Sea and the Black Sea [Map 70] of 1610. Colour-coded to help sailors distinguish territories, it is an example of the progress in Dutch cartography in the sixteenth century.

World Map, 1529.
Diego Ribeiro.
Parchment, 85 x 204.5 cm.
Biblioteca Apostolica Vaticana, Vatican.
(Map 37)

*The Boke of Idrography
(Oriental India)*, 1542.
Jean Rotz. Paper, 59.5 x 77 cm.
The British Library, London. (Map 39)

Explorers' Lifelines

Discovering New Worlds, West and East: 1400-1500

Spa	Martin Pinzón	[c.1441–1493]
Itl	John Cabot	[c.1450–1499]
Itl	Christopher Columbus	[c.1451–1506]
Itl	Amerigo Vespucci	[1455–1512]
Spa	Juan Sebastian del Canto	[c.1460–1526]
Spa	Vicente Pinzón	[c.1460–c.1523]
Por	Vasco da Gama	[1460–1524]
Spa	Juan Ponce de León	[1460–1521]
Por	Pedro Alvarez Cabral	[c.1467–1520]
Por	Bartolomeu Dias	[?–1500]
Spa	Pánfilo de Narváez	[1470–1528]
Spa	Bartolomé de Las Casas	[1474–1566]

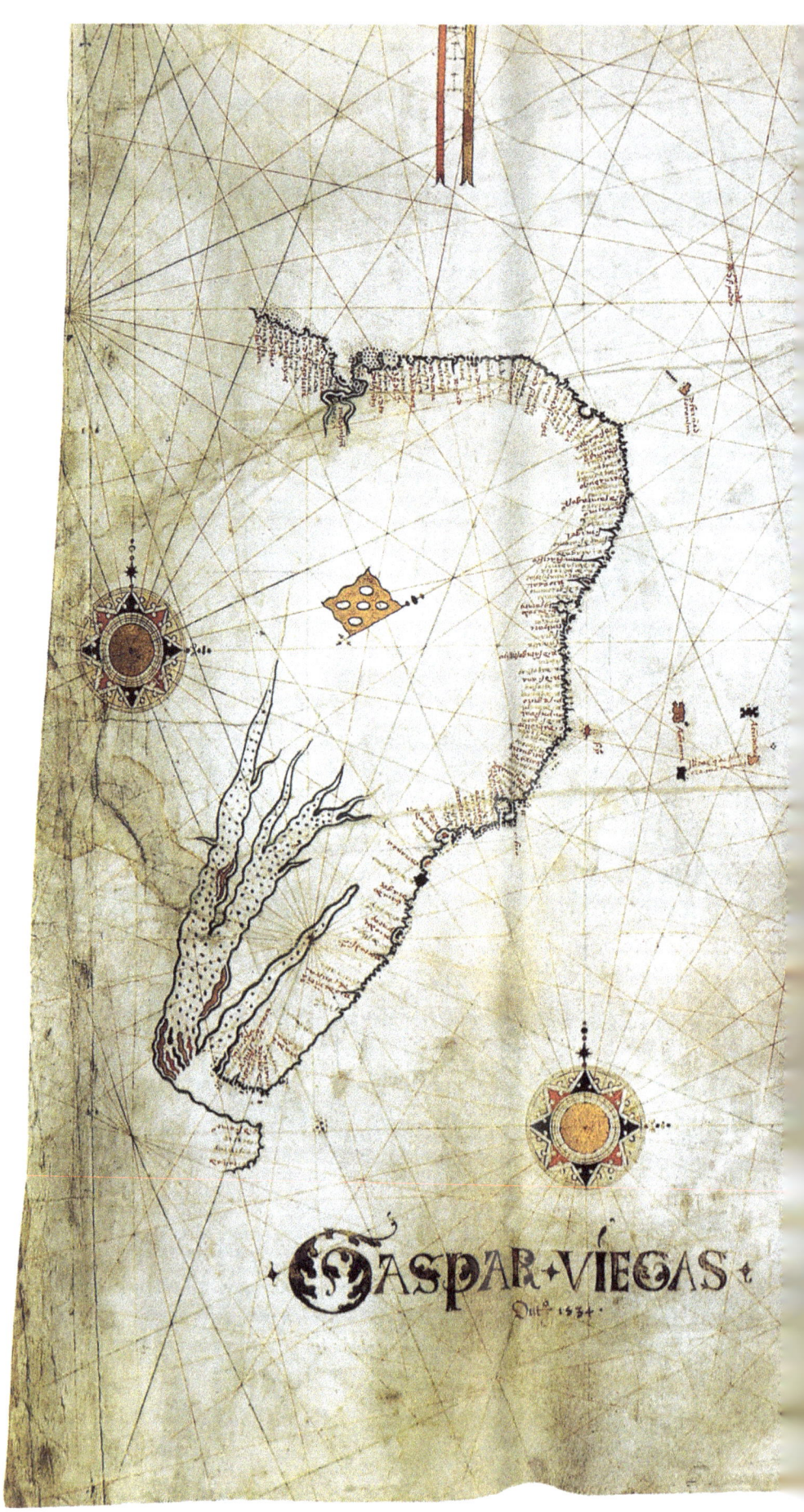

Atlantic Ocean, 1534.
Gaspar Viegas.
Parchment, 70 x 96 cm.
Bibliothèque nationale de France,
Paris. (Map 38)

CHAPTER III

BEYOND THE NEW WORLD: 1500 – 1550

Vasco De Balboa

The Spanish conquistador most identified with personal independence is undoubtedly Vasco Núñez de Balboa. While he is best known as the first European to see the Pacific Ocean from the Americas, he is rarely noted for his other achievements or his tragic end. Popular misconceptions surrounding him include the notion that he named both Panama and the Pacific Ocean.

After coming to the New World on a supply ship at about the age of twenty-five, Balboa became a farmer but was soon in debt. In an effort both to escape his creditors and avoid extradition to Spain, he smuggled himself aboard a ship bound from Hispaniola for Colombia.

During a stopover in Cartagena, Balboa happened to meet Francisco Pizarro, who was to play an important role in the rest of his life. He went with Pizarro to Darién, the isthmus that we now know as Panama. In what would prove to be Balboa's good fortune, they landed near the narrow segment of the continent; he was only a few miles east of the great body of water described to him by the natives.

In the Spanish colony in Darién, Balboa managed to wrest control from the governor appointed by King Ferdinand II of Aragon. As the self-appointed head of the village, he acquired native guides to help him travel west through the jungle.

Shortly before reaching his goal, Balboa and his men encountered Indians in the area whom they first fought off, killing only in self-defence, but then proceeded to capture and torture other natives, apparently to intimidate the rest.

The Boke of Idrography (Atlantic Ocean), 1542.
Jean Rotz.
Paper, 59.5 x 77 cm.
The British Library, London.
(Map 40)

The Southern Sea

From a hilltop near the west coast on 17 September 1513, Balboa was the first European to see the Pacific from the Americas. Even though his expedition had been undertaken without the express approval of Spain, he carried the Spanish flag into the water and claimed not only the ocean for Spain but also all the islands surrounded by it.

Other Europeans, notably Marco Polo in the late fifteenth century, had reported seeing the ocean off Asia, but the idea in Europe that this was an ocean distinct from the Atlantic dates only back to Balboa's sighting. He named the ocean the Southern Sea. We will see that it was later Ferdinand Magellan who named it the Pacific Ocean.

During Balboa's return east through the Darién jungle to the village, he kidnapped Tubanama, a tribal chief, and held him for ransom. (It may be that the name Panama derives from the European pronunciation of Tubanama.)

Meanwhile, Spain had appointed a new official governor of Darién, who did not approve of the ambitious shipbuilding enterprise established by Balboa. In order to venture into the Pacific, Balboa envisioned needing at least two caravels. He built these ships on the west coast of the isthmus with the aid of natives he had hired for that purpose.

Observing the shipbuilding and the growing influence of the enterprising conquistador, the new governor suspected the rogue of trying to establish his own independent province. Eventually the governor inveigled Francisco Pizarro into bringing his friend Balboa back to Darién, where he was taken into custody.

Balboa undoubtedly committed some serious crimes during his exploits, but he was not a traitor – the crime for which he was convicted. He was beheaded in 1519.

Francisco Pizarro

Before the initial and accidental meeting with Balboa in Cartagena, his fellow-conquistador Francisco Pizarro was with the expeditions of Nicolas de Ovando and Alonso de Ojeda (see above).

But like Balboa he probably always had his own agenda. His personal quest was to acquire the legendary riches of the Incas, which had been described to him by the Indians in Panama. After his first and unsuccessful attempt to steal gold

Francisco Pizarro, Sailor and Conquistador, 1835.
Amable-Paul Coutan (1792-1837).
Oil on canvas, 73 x 58 cm.
Château de Versailles, Versailles.

World Map, 1543.
Battista Agnese.
Parchment, 19.5 x 29.5 cm.
Bibliothèque nationale de France, Paris. (Map 41)

Rigged Model of a Portuguese Caravela from c.1535.
Wood.
Science Museum, London.

Naval Steerage,
Adam Silo (1674-1760).
Oil on canvas.
The State Hermitage Museum, St Petersburg.

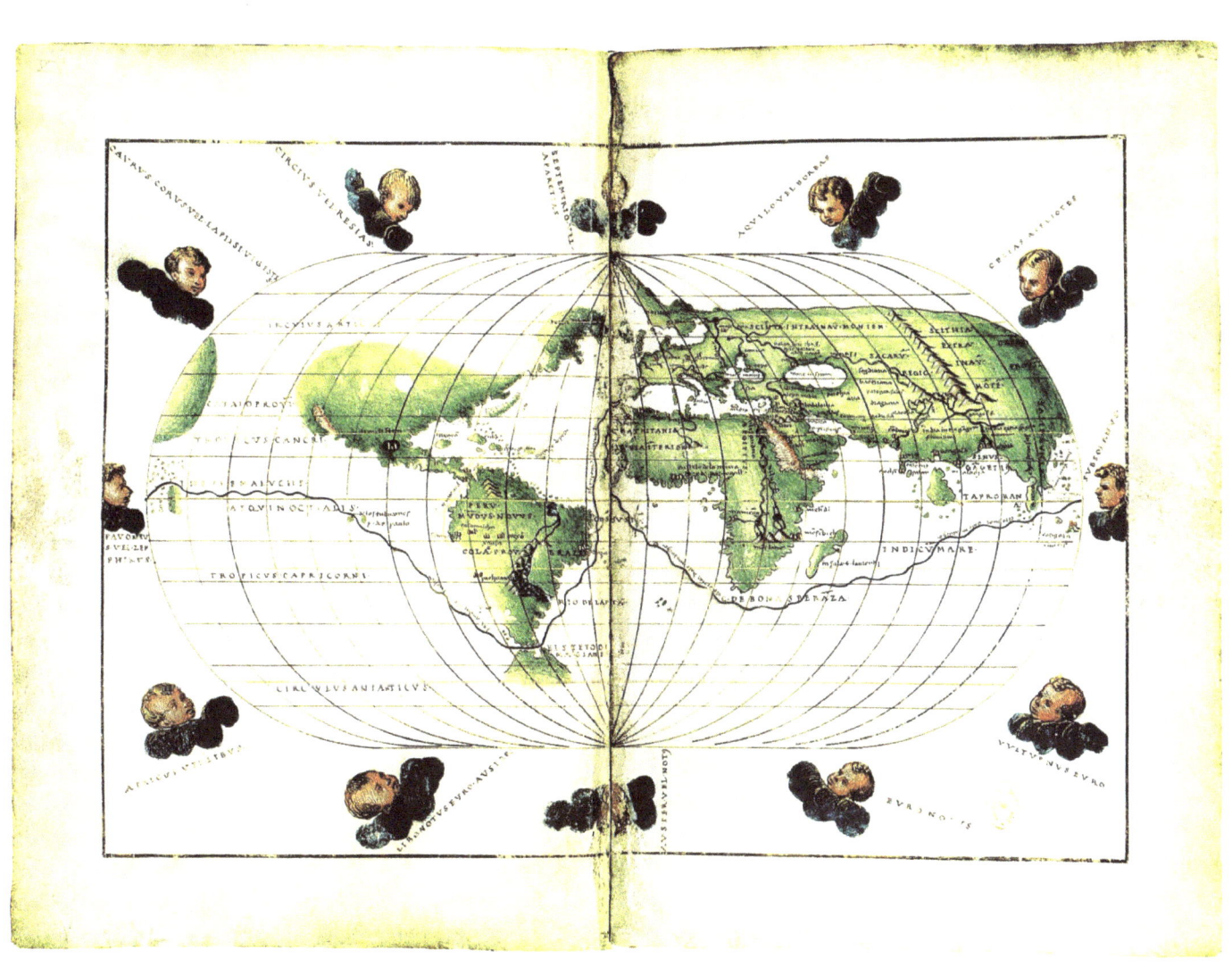

THE CARAVEL

Although the *Santa Maria* – the flagship of Columbus' trio of ships – and the ships of Magellan were never recovered and there is no detailed description of them, reconstructions have been made of the kind of ship we know them to have been.

The *Santa Maria*, for example, was a caravel, a class originally used for coastal trade and short trips. It was the kind of ship that was surely more often used for the initial exploration that helped gather data for portolani.

However, after design improvements the caravel was found to be also capable of much longer trips.

Because the early caravels that made transatlantic voyages were built in Europe, we might think of them as being constructed only there.

However, Francisco Pizarro, Vasco de Balboa, and other explorers built small versions of caravels in the Americas.

while in Peru, his second expedition in 1526 reached Ecuador, where he looted all the gold he could from the natives.

With him at the time was his business partner, Diego de Almagro. (About fifteen years later it would be Almagro's son who would murder Pizarro.)

In 1529, Pizarro returned to Spain carrying gold together with enticing descriptions of the amazing wealth of the Incas. The conquistador was given permission and authority to invade and plunder the Inca Empire in the name of Spain, even though his brutality was known to all at the time.

After sailing back to the new continent and braving almost overwhelming difficulties, Pizarro led his army south through the jungle. Although the Incas did not yet have the wheel, they had developed excellent paths and bridges.

Ironically these helped their invaders move quickly through the Andes mountains to conquer them.

After bloody battles with the Incas, Pizarro needed to reinforce his diminishing troops. Hernando de Soto was one of the men who joined Pizarro two years later when bringing new troops to the seriously depleted invaders. (The very ambitious de Soto would go on to discover the Mississippi in 1541.)

At the time of Pizarro's invasion, the Inca Empire was already in the midst of a civil war, a chaotic situation that Pizarro exploited by capturing and holding for an immense ransom the king of one of the two warring factions. After many battles, Lima became the conqueror's new capital city in 1535, even though pockets of resistance continued for decades. In the wake of their ordeal, the conquistadors reserved only a fifth of the vast treasure they obtained for their king back in Spain; they kept the remaining loot to themselves.

Ferdinand Magellan

As schoolchildren we were routinely taught that the navigator Ferdinand Magellan was the first to circumnavigate the globe. We might now learn how that statement is not accurate.

Magellan was a page at the court of King Manuel I from the age of fifteen to twenty-four. No doubt with the inspiring stories of the recent conquests of da Gama and Cabral fresh in mind, he joined an armada in 1504 that destroyed the fleets of Egypt and India, making Portugal at least as dominant as Spain as a power on the high seas (see above).

World Map, 1534.
Guillaume Brouscon.
Parchment, 64 x 45 cm.
Henry E. Huntington Library and Art Gallery,
Saint Marine. (Map 42)

Portrait of Ferdinand Magellan.
António Menendez.
Museu Marinha, Lisbon.

In spite of Magellan's life of service to his liege lord up till then, including being seriously wounded in battle, he was undoubtedly even more wounded in a non-physical sense by accusations of illegal activity brought against him at court – charges that later were, however, dropped.

Perhaps because of this slap in the face, Magellan renounced his Portuguese citizenship and turned to Charles I of Spain, from whom he won sponsorship for his truly amazing and somewhat risky plan. Magellan convinced the young King Charles that he could reach the Southern Sea by sailing west. It would be the most ambitious exploration project ever. (We will see, below, the vital role Charles played in the Age of Discovery.)

At that time, though, there was no proof that a passage from the Atlantic to the Pacific existed. Some contemporary scholars thought a North-west Passage seemed a more likely solution.

Spain was very interested in participating in the lucrative commerce with India and the Spice Islands. However, the 1494 Treaty of Tordesillas gave her rival Portugal access to those markets from the east, a possibility that was used successfully by da Gama and later by Cabral.

To be able to reach the Spice Islands by sailing west would be like going through the back door of a house that they were forbidden to enter through the front door. (We will see how several years later a papal amendment to the treaty significantly changed the rules and the political geography thereafter.)

Magellan's confidence came from years of navigational research. Cartographers and other mariners had proposed to Magellan that there might be a route around the southern tip of the New World.

He had also befriended the astronomer Rui Faleiro, who shared with Magellan his unique insights about calculating latitude, even though, before John 'Longitude' Harrison's chronometer (see p. 64), there was still no reliable way of determining longitude. That was a problem that neither Newton nor Galileo had conquered.

It was originally intended that Faleiro would accompany Magellan, but he dropped out of the project, partly because he thought there were astrological warnings against his doing so. Belief in astrology was so pervasive at the time that Pope Sixtus V officially condemned the occult science in 1595. The work of the astrologer Nostradamus in France had become both popular and influential in the previous century; secular prophecy was threatening the Church's control over spiritual matters.

Pilot Manual for the Use of Breton Mariners (Atlantic Maps), 1548. Guillaume Brouscon. Parchment, 27.5 x 31 cm. Bibliothèque nationale de France, Paris. (Map 43)

The First Voyage Around the World

The equipment Magellan took with him included twenty-four portolani, or parchment maps, as well as a number of compasses, quadrants, astrolabes, hourglasses, and a copy of Faleiro's work on latitude. We will explain below why all of these very valuable objects amazingly were deliberately thrown overboard by Magellan himself.

We know of such details thanks to one of the crew, Antonio Pigafetta, who in 1525 published a beautifully illuminated journal that has been used, along with the accounts of other survivors, to create a blow-by-blow account of the expedition.

Tension was assured from the outset of the expedition because most of the officers were Portuguese (as was Magellan by birth), whereas most of the crew were Spanish. That would prove to be one of Magellan's greatest mistakes.

After only a few days into the Atlantic, one of the very small number of officers who was Spanish – Juan de Cartagena – was arrested and imprisoned on board for planning a mutiny with some of the Spanish crew. During a later mutiny attempt headed by another rebellious officer, de Cartagena was freed.

However, during both episodes the majority of the crew remained loyal to Magellan. The second treasonable officer was executed. De Cartagena escaped with his life – but as punishment was marooned on the inhospitable coast of Patagonia (in southern Argentina).

During his voyage southward along the South American coast, Magellan noticed the mouth of a channel, but of course had no way of knowing how far inland it went. He sent one of his ships into the channel to scout, but the crew was afraid to navigate further than the outlying strait.

It was not unusual at that time for intelligent people still to believe in sea monsters. (The illustrations on portolani of the period often show images of fantastic creatures intended to be terrifying in the lands and in the waters of regions yet to be explored.) Having spotted penguins and other unfamiliar creatures for the first time, rumors of sea monsters spread through the superstitious sailors of the expedition. Instead of sailing west, the crew that was meant to be scouting ahead deserted and sailed their ship back to Spain.

Pilot Manual for the Use of Breton Mariners (Quadrante of the Drizzles, Le Havre to Mores Maps), 1548.
Guillaume Brouscon.
Parchment, 17.5 x 14 cm.
Bibliothèque nationale de France, Paris. (Map 44)

The Strait of Magellan

It was up to Magellan himself then to carefully navigate the remaining ships through the difficult 563-kilometre waterway as they discovered what they had hoped for – a navigable passage to the Southern Sea. The passage would soon be called the Strait of Magellan. Meanwhile, Magellan called the ocean they reached 'Pacific', for its relative calm, compared to the turbulent waters through which he had just passed.

During that historic 1521 voyage, Magellan pressed west across the ocean. Nobody knows exactly the route he took. Because the voyage was taking much longer than anyone expected and rations had been used up, the crew grew restless, trusting the maps and their instruments less and less. In a calculated act of bravado designed to avoid a final mutiny, Magellan called the crew together to watch as he dramatically threw his navigational tools and maps overboard, implying that he, like the crew, trusted more in God than in science.

Eventually the fleet made landfall in 1521 on the island of Samar in the group of islands that would later be renamed the Philippines. Unfortunately for him, Magellan was so intent on trying to spread Christianity that he delayed his search for gold: his first priority was apparently to force the natives into instant conversion. And a final mistake was to attack a local chief who refused to be converted. After losing that skirmish, Magellan was killed while retreating.

The first few successors to Magellan were also killed before a new leader was voted in to head up the expedition. Even then the crew apparently engaged in pirate-like looting.

Eventually, Juan Sebastian del Cano was chosen to continue the voyage, not knowing that their journey around the globe was to take seventeen more months before arriving back in Spain in 1522, three years after their departure.

The Victoria was the first of Magellan's ships to return to Spain, but each of the other four ships of the fleet had its own adventure. For example, the original flagship, the Trinidad, first attempted to return to Spain from the Southern Sea by sailing north-east over the north of North America. Unprepared for the cold weather of the far north, it was forced to return to the Spice Islands.

A second ship survived the expedition only for its Spanish crew to be imprisoned by the Portuguese, dramatically illustrating that the quarrelling peoples of the world were still not united even though humanity had just become much closer because of the circumnavigation.

Atlantic Ocean, after 1549. (c. 1550).
Unknown artist.
Parchment, 88 x 63 cm.
Bibliothèque nationale de France, Paris. (Map 45)

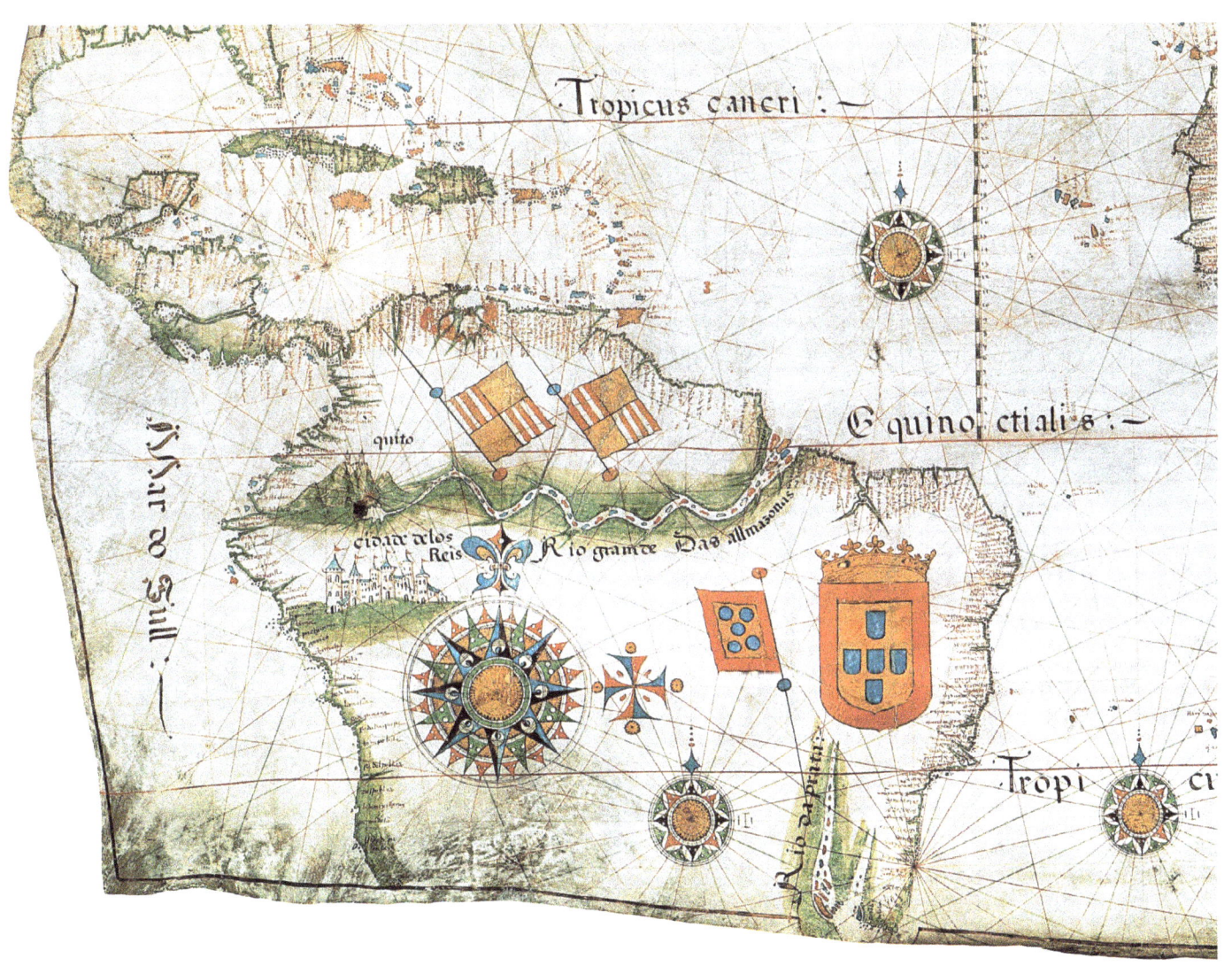

Charles I, King of Spain

After the death of his grandfather Ferdinand II, a young man named Charles became Charles I, King of Spain in 1516, and three years later he also became Charles V of the Holy Roman Empire. At his death nearly half a century later he was undoubtedly the most dominant political authority in Europe since Charlemagne. And he was called by many, especially by his conquistadors, 'the ruler of the world'.

Atlantic Ocean, 1550.
Diego Gutierrez.
Parchment stuck onto paper,
131.8 x 88.5 cm.
Bibliothèque nationale
de France, Paris. (Map 46)

Charles' amazing success in defending his Habsburg realm (Austria) against France, the Ottoman Turks, and the recently formed German Protestants led many people – including himself – to think he was divinely appointed to be 'God's standard-bearer', and to spread Christianity to the world.

World Map, 1550.
Pierre Desceliers.
Parchment, 135 x 215 cm.
The British Museum, London.
(Map 47)

For many years, even after the start of the Protestant Reformation, Christianity still meant only Catholicism to most Europeans.

The heraldic motto of Charles – *Plus Ultra* (Further and further) – inspired especially his Spanish subjects to try to spread Christianity to the world.

His involvement in aggressive conquest – most notably by the Spaniards of territories in the Americas – helped change forever the political face of the globe. The achievement of Magellan's fleet, which had received its mandate from Charles I, was motivated a great deal by such apostolic zeal. Again, much of all exploration during the Age of Discovery was for 'God, glory, or greed', or (to put it another way) 'converts, conquests, and commerce'.

In his books, map expert Dr Peter Whitfield reminds us to qualify how we consider the conquistadors and others who were not motivated primarily by exploring. He stresses, 'To speak of Cortés, or Pizarro, as explorers is like describing them as reformers of indigenous governments. Their motive was conquest and plunder, which they achieved with ruthless success, but in the process they gained, incidentally, a place in the history of exploration.'[23]

Jacques Cartier Discovering the Saint Laurent River in Canada in 1535, 1847. Jean Antoine Théodore de Gudin (1802-1880). Oil on canvas, 142 x 266 cm. Château de Versailles, Versailles.

HERNAN CORTES

Hernán Cortés was a university student for only two years before dropping out. After two years of leisurely travel, he decided at the age of nineteen in

1504 to seek his fame and fortune in the New World. He sailed to Santo Domingo and soon participated in the conquest of Cuba by the conquistador Diego de Velázquez de Cuéllar.

By 1519 he was ready to lead his own expedition, and duly set out to invade Mexico, where he founded a city near today's Veracruz. He deceptively befriended the enemies of the Aztecs by claiming to be Quetzalcóatl, a legendary ruler and messiah-figure that Aztec legend held would return to Mexico from the east.

Scholars are not certain if the ruler took his name from the god or if he was revered as a god himself [see illustration 40], but we do know that 'Montezuma II believed Cortés to be a deity because he had landed in Mexico on the day of One Reed, the calendar date of Quetzalcóatl's birthday.'[24]

Believing in the legend and apparently also in the unconscionable claim of Cortés, the gullible Aztec king Montezuma II allowed Cortés to take over the Aztec capital, Tenochtitlán (now Mexico City) (see p. 128).

Portrait of Hernán Cortés. Biblioteca Nacional de España, Madrid.

The World (Florida), 1556. Guillaume Le Testu. Paper, 37 x 53 cm. Service historique de l'Armée de Terre, Vincennes. (Map 48)

Spaniard Against Spaniard

Apparently to secure his own claim, Cortés also had to fight rival Spaniards. Returning to the capital from defeating an army led by the conquistador Pánfilo de Narváez, he found the Aztecs in revolt. He was forced to withdraw his troops

The World (The New France), 1556.
Guillaume Le Testu.
Paper, 37 x 53 cm.
Service historique de l'Armée de Terre,
Vincennes. (Map 49)

The World (Terra Nova), 1556.
Guillaume Le Testu.
Paper, 37 x 53 cm.
Service historique de l'Armée de Terre, Vincennes. (Map 50)

from the city but was able to return about a year later and easily retake it because its population was by then plagued by an epidemic disease.

By 1521 Cortés had finally conquered the Aztec Empire through political as well as military skills. And just as he had originally exploited the superstitions of the natives, he later also took advantage of their tragic misfortune. After granting himself large areas of land, Cortés distributed the rest of the spoils of their plundering between his men.

Returning to Spain, Cortés was honored for his exploits. Later, he was involved in expeditions to Honduras and Baja California, as well as in an unsuccessful attack on Algiers.

The Arrival of Hernán Cortés in Mexico, 16th century. Anonymous, Spanish school. Oil on canvas. Museo de América, Madrid.

JACQUES CARTIER

In 1533, after Francis I of France had managed to convince Pope Clement VII to amend the 1494 Treaty of Tordesillas, the French were once again permitted to

explore the New World. Generally ignoring the rights of indigenous peoples, the amendment granted ownership of newly discovered land to whichever nation reached and claimed it first.

The distinction between religion and politics remained unclear, and it was the practice of Jacques Cartier – as it was of Columbus, Magellan, Balboa, and many other Christian explorers – to erect a cross whenever he claimed territory for his sponsor or on behalf of his own native land (see above).

Cartier's original aim was, as it had been for a number of Europeans before him, to find the North-west Passage to the Far East. In 1535, on the Feast of Saint Lawrence (10 August), Cartier reached a bay he named after the saint. With the help of local natives the mouth of the major river that flowed into the bay was found days later. Cartier called the river simply La Grande Rivière. The entire Gulf of St Lawrence and the St Lawrence River were given their names later by others.

After a winter of illness and hardship in the colony he established, Cartier needed to return home for supplies and men. He obliged the local Huron chief and some

The Battle of Tepeaca,
16th century.
Anonymous, Spanish school.
Oil on canvas.
Museo de América,
Madrid.

other natives to return with him to France, apparently both to prove that he had indeed reached this new territory and in order to teach the Indians French.

When he got back again to the colony, the Hurons there were falsely told that their chief had died 'of a surfeit of good living', and that the other Hurons who had gone to France preferred to stay there, and were living in luxury. In fact all but one were already dead.

Cartier's voyage inland as far as present day Montreal was the foundation for France's later claim to Canada. The political landscape of North America would be thereafter influenced by the explorations of his small group of men.

Cartier's Second Voyage

After Cartier put together 1,000 men and five ships for a second voyage, Francis I placed Jean-François de Roberval in command, with Cartier as his lieutenant. However, a high price was paid for Cartier lost twenty-five of his men to scurvy before discovering a local remedy, a brew made from the bark of white cedar. (The effective use of vitamin C in limes to prevent scurvy was not discovered before James Cook's expeditions.) During the final expedition, thirty-five others were killed, apparently by Iroquois.

Minerals brought back from the colonies that Cartier hoped were precious gems turned out instead to be worthless. And the St Lawrence proved not to be the North-west Passage. But although Cartier achieved none of his goals, at least – unlike those of a number explorers of his day – his death in 1537 was not violent.

The writings of Jacques Cartier describe in detail his three voyages of exploration to North America and especially his being the European discoverer of the St Lawrence River in 1534. Yet his works give few autobiographical details.

We do not know, for example, if he was, as some conjecture, with Giovanni da Verrazano as part of an early expedition to America in 1524.

PORTOLANI DURING THIS PERIOD

Maps (similar to Maps 22–44) available to Frobisher, Drake and Davis and their contemporaries in the sixteenth century could have been available, although of course it is unlikely that many of the pirate and privateer maps of the time were made public.

The World (Java), 1556. Guillaume Le Testu. Paper, 37 x 53 cm. Service historique de l'Armée de Terre, Vincennes. (Map 51)

The actual maps available to such 'unofficial' navigators were certainly more sophisticated than, for example, the treasure map imagined later by the illustrators of Robert Louis Stevenson's classic Treasure Island (1883).

The Portuguese School

In this collection there are twenty-three examples of the Portugese school at Lisbon (c. 1470–1706): Maps 25, 27, 29–34, 45, 52–54, 55, 59, 63, 73, 81, 82, 85, 86, 94. Others show the influence of the Genovese school [Maps 2–6, 21, 23, 24, 26, 41, 56]. They influenced most subsequent schools of the sixteenth and seventeenth centuries.

Of these, the Normandy, Japanese, and French schools were seriously influenced, while the Spanish and English schools were influenced less directly.

In Map 17 the nomenclature is in several Mediterranean languages. On each non-Muslim city between Ceuta and Venice, a banner identifies the city as Christian, reflecting the influence of the Crusades. The row of tents pictured in Africa are similar to those on the 1563 map by Giacomo de Maggiolo [Map 56].

The maps 29–34 of the *Miller Atlante* are so named after their last owner. This atlas, considered a major work of art as well as significant source of maritime information, is unfortunately now incomplete.

It once covered the entire known world before the Magellan discoveries. Portuguese banners on the maps show the important markets or new discoveries of that nation. The miniatures of native birds, animals and fauna were done by Gregorio Lopes. The content shows the influence of Ptolemy's *Geographia*. Each map has a rhumb-line system with sixteen secondary centers, a distance scale, and red lines to indicate the equator and the tropics.

Another Portuguese map of the Lisbon school is the anonymous map of the Atlantic made after 1549. Map 45 exhibits the coats of arms and banners typical of major political landowners.

The portolani of Diogo Homem [Maps 52–54] and his brother Andreas Homem [Map 55] would seem to reflect the influence of their father Lopo Homem, official cartographer to the King of Portugal. Their works are dated 1559.

The work of Andreas is the only one now known, whereas Diogo was possibly the most prolific Portuguese cartographer of his century, creating at least a dozen universal or Mediterranean atlases and eleven large maps. It would also seem,

Atlas (Occidental Europe), 1559.
Diogo Homem.
Parchment, 44 x 58.6 cm.
Bibliothèque nationale de France, Paris. (Map 52)

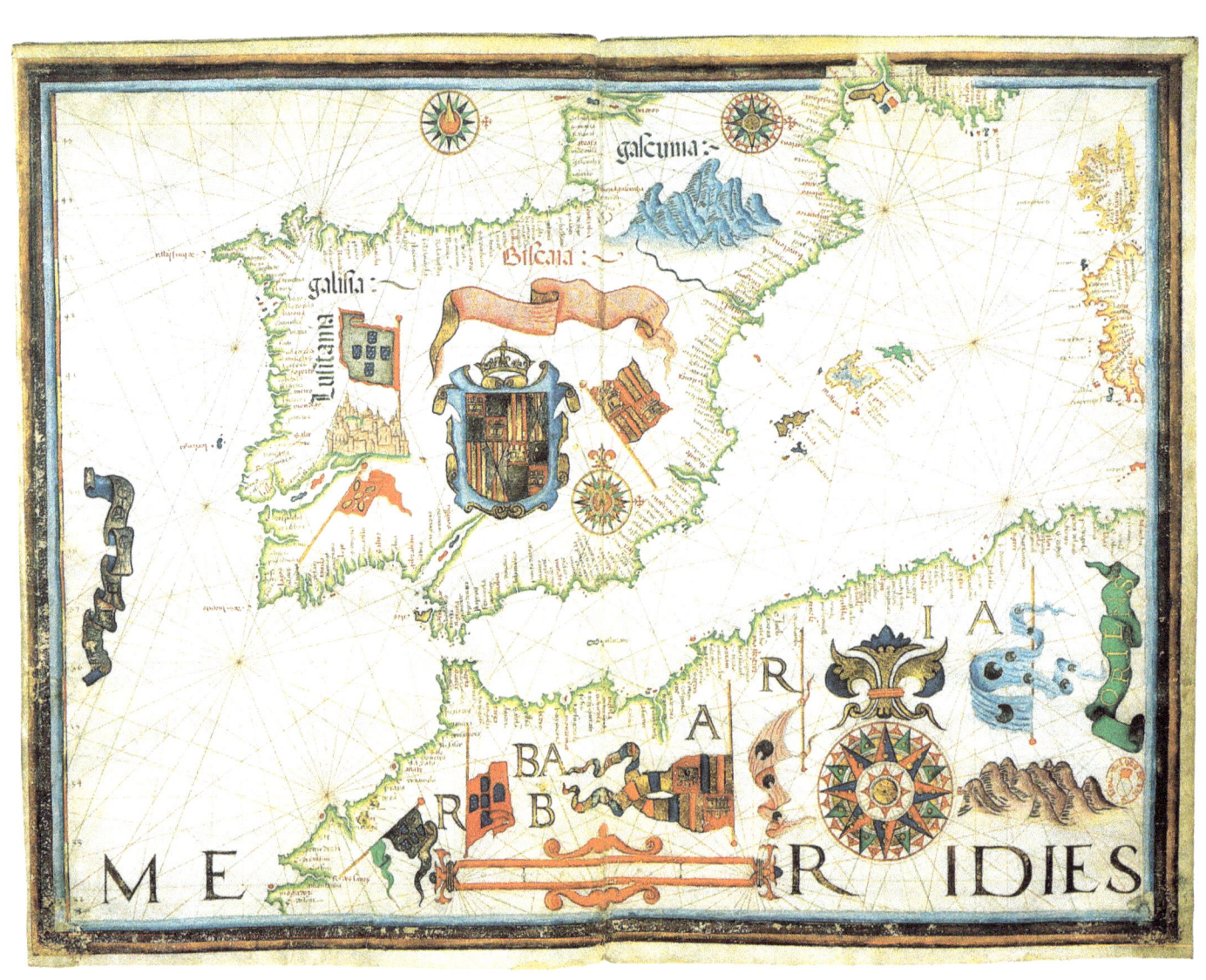

Atlas (Oriental Atlantic and Occidental Mediterranean), 1559. Diogo Homem.
Parchment, 44 x 58.6 cm.
Bibliothèque nationale de France, Paris.
(Map 53)

Atlas (Black Sea), 1559.
Diogo Homem.
Parchment, 44 x 58.6 cm.
Bibliothèque nationale de France, Paris.
(Map 54)

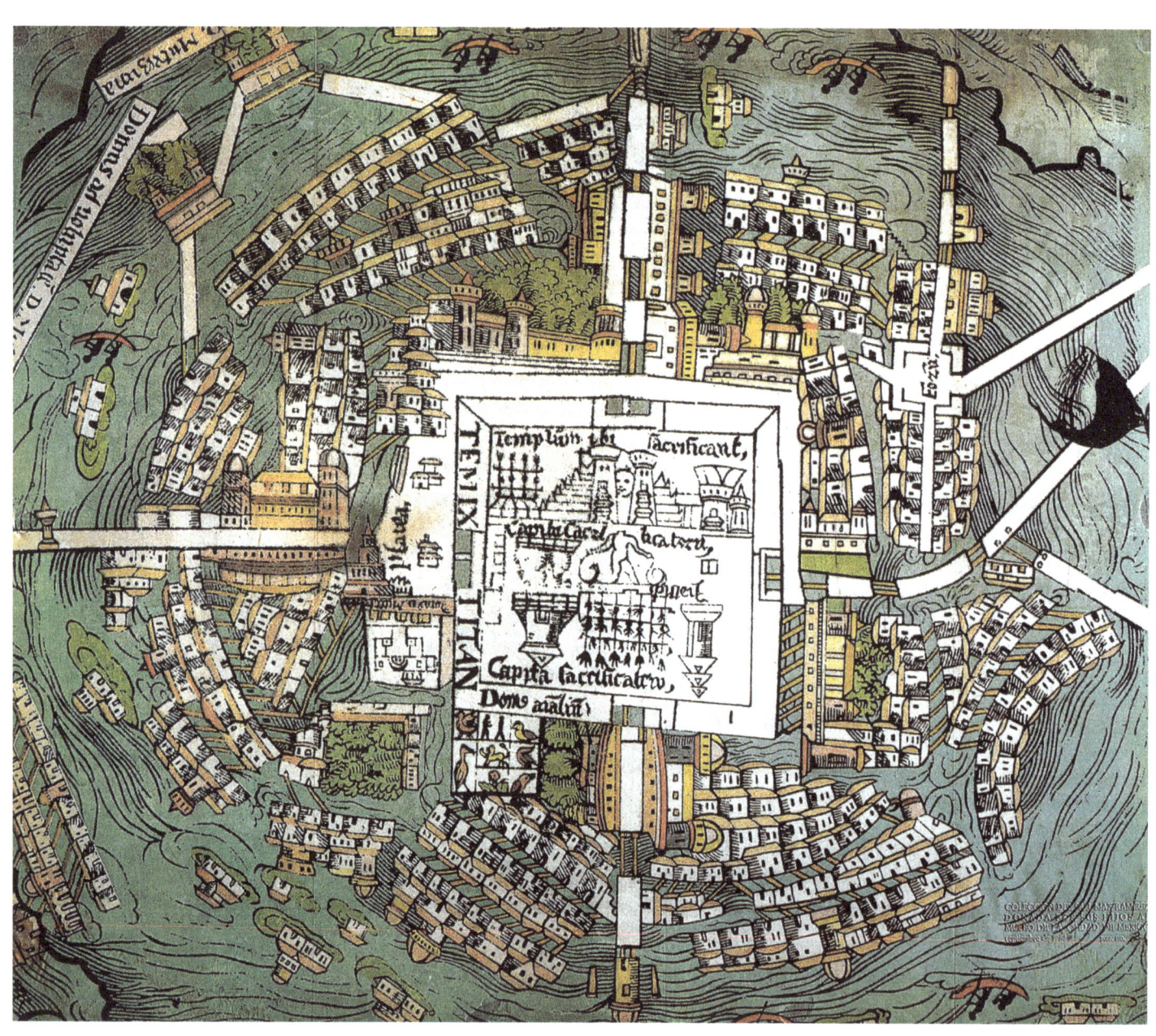

Copy of the Map of Tenochtitlán, by Hernán Cortés (1485-1547), from Praeclara Ferdinandi Cortesii de Nova maris Hyspania narratio, 1524. Private collection.

then, that the one brother created a large number of works, while the other may have been responsible for only one truly huge work. Andreas' ten parchment sheets comprise two rows of five sections making the resulting work the largest Portuguese nautical map of the Renaissance.

His map displays a certain freedom from the limitations of Ptolemy's work. It shows the division of the known world markets into two parts according to the Treaty of Tordesillas: the Spanish to the west and the Portuguese to the east.

The portolano of the Atlantic and the Mediterranean by Giacomo de Maggiolo [Map 56] shows that he used a recent edition of Ptolemy's *Geographia*, at least when presenting Denmark and the Scandinavian Peninsula. But in this 1563 work there is also a new awareness of northern Europe. The Madonna and the infant Jesus are respectfully centered on the left side of the map.

The anonymous Portuguese universal map [Map 63] attributed by the French to Pedro de Lemos was drawn up in around 1585. It includes, probably for the first time, the Philippine archipelago. Each hemisphere has its own rhumb-line system. The influence of the Treaty of Tondesillas is seen on the map in the division of the world between the Spanish and the Portuguese.

The 1618 Atlantic Map [Map 73] is the only known map of Domingos Sanchez. Patron saints are represented, especially St Joseph with the infant Jesus, also Saints Benedict, Leonard, Stephen and Barbara.

The Monomotapa Empire, south of the current Zimbabwe, was occupied by the Portuguese then by the Arabs from the fifteenth century to the nineteenth century. On the map of João Teixeira Albernas II (1677), the gold mines in the area are indicated. Portuguese merchants had their own security forces that regulated the circulation of gold and defied local authorities. The map-maker was well known following the publication of his 1665 atlas showing the African coasts. Years later, these maps were included in a work published in 1700 in Amsterdam.

Aztec Prince in Ceremonial Dress, illustration by Diego Durán, *Historia de las Indias de Nueva España e Islas de Tierra Firme*, 1579.
Drawing coloured with gouache.
Biblioteca Nacional de España, Madrid.

The Spanish School

These portolani [Maps 22, 46] of the Spanish school at Seville (1508-1709) show the influence of fourteenth-century Catalunia.

The Genovese and Viennese Schools

The important map of Juan de la Cosa [Map 22] is discussed in some detail above. The map of the Atlantic by Diego Gutierrez of 1550 [Map 46] employs a system of two gradations in latitude, but these were soon found to be impractical. In fact, Ferdinand Columbus, the son of Christopher, and Jean Rotz denounced these maps, saying they were merely confusing to seafarers.

The Istanbul School

Portolani 28, 35, 36 from the school centered in Istanbul (1513-1601) show the influence of the early examples of the Viennese school [Maps 10, 11, 15, 18, 19], while their style was not passed on to other major schools.

Piri Re'is, the author of the *Turkish Map of the Atlantic* [Map 28] in 1513, was born in 1470. His uncle had been a pirate but was later a multilingual commodore in the Ottoman navy at the end of the fifteenth century, who wrote an influential study of sixteenth-century Mediterranean cartography. His nephew's map was discovered in 1929 during the reconstruction of the Topkapi Museum. The map shows only the eastern part of a larger and lost planisphere.

The two illuminated documents [Maps 35 and 36] from a Turkish instruction book were also drawn up by Piri Re'is in about 1525-1526. The book comprised no fewer than 848 pages which included 215 nautical maps. Before its publication, many of the details it gives of the Mediterranean Sea had never been described.

The Normandy School

In this presentation there are fourteen examples of portolani of the Normandy school centered at Dieppe (1536-1635): Maps 39, 40, 47-51, 58, 79, 61, 67, 71, 78, 80, and 84. These show the direct influence of the Portuguese school, and they in turn influenced the later English school in London (1579-1701) and thereafter the French school in Paris (1661-1751). Pierre Desceliers' universal

Universa ac navigabilis totius terrarum orbis descriptio, 1559.
Etreas Homem.
Parchment stuck onto paper, 150 x 294 cm.
Bibliothèque nationale de France, Paris. (Map 55)

World Map, 1566.
Nicolas Desliens.
Parchment, 27 x 45 cm.
Bibliothèque nationale de France, Paris. (Map 58)

Atlantic Ocean and Mediterranean Sea, 1563.
Giacomo de Maggiolo.
Parchment stuck onto parchment sheet, 102.3 x 85 cm.
Bibliothèque nationale de France, Paris. (Map 56)

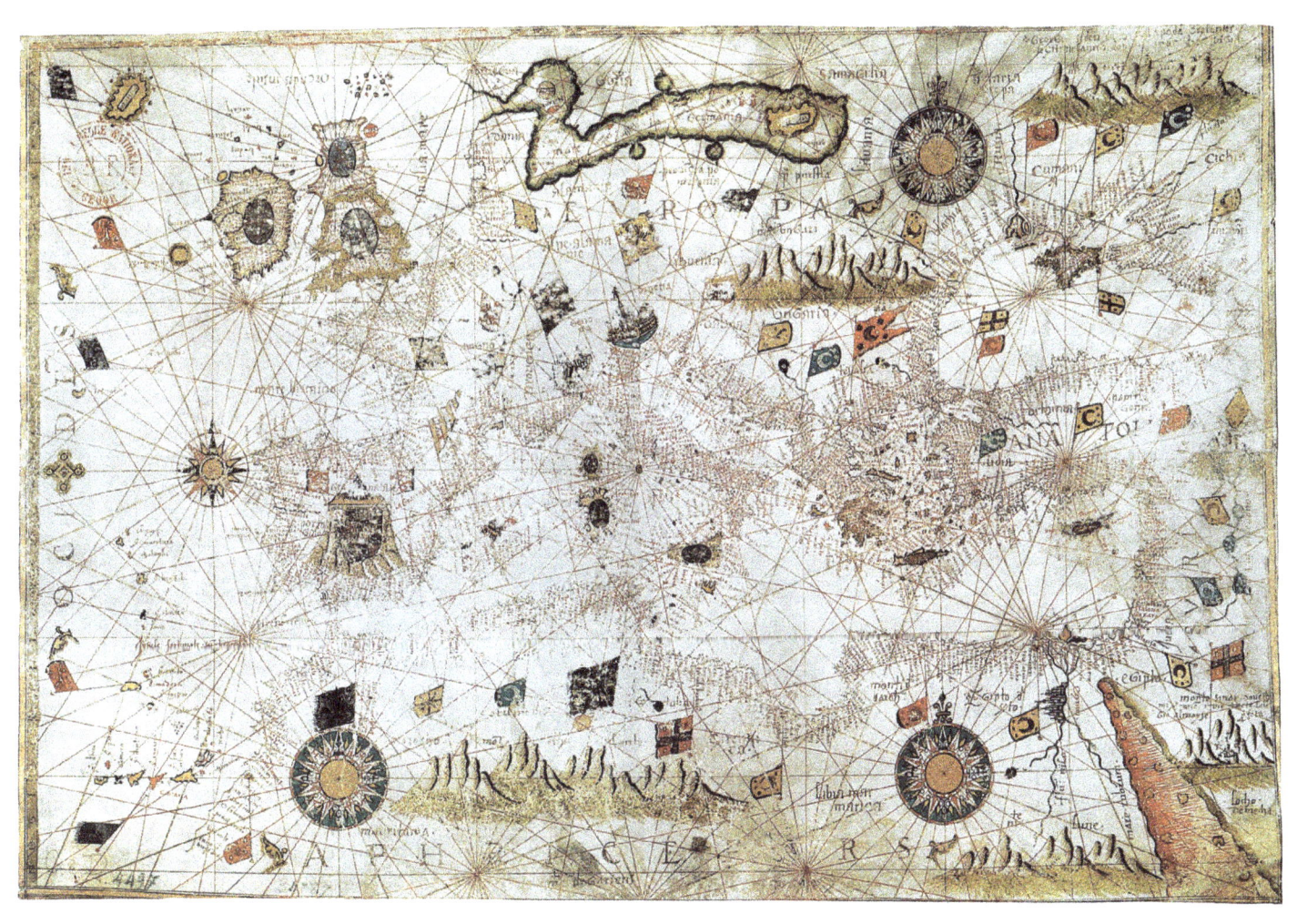

The Mediterranean Basin, 1565.
Giorgio Sideri (known as Calapoda).
Parchment, 29 x 43 cm.
Bibliothèque nationale de France,
Paris. (Map 57)

map [Map 47] uses a 'walk-around' format. On the left appear the twelve climates of the Ptolemaic system, from the equator to the poles.

Four universal maps by Guillaume Le Testu [Maps 48-51] from Normandy in the sixteenth century reflect the discoveries of Cartier. Scholars note that these maps perpetuate some of the errors of the Portuguese maps, but are an improvement over those of Rotz [Maps 39, 40].

The universal map of Nicolas Desliens [Map 58] brings together all that was known at Dieppe at the time. This map, like many during the Renaissance, is oriented to the south (with north at the bottom of the map).

The only known portolani of Jacques de Vau de Claye are the two [Maps 60, 61] dated 1579. They show the Portuguese influence even though the nomenclature is in French. These are multi-purpose maps: nautical charts in that coasts are detailed, economic maps in that products (gold, amber, wood, sugar, cotton) are indicated, anthropological maps in that the local Indian population is shown in their native dress, and natural history maps in that rare birds and monkeys are illustrated.

There is also a military purpose in showing the conquest of the Brazilian coast as imagined by Catherine de Medici (1519-1589), but her aim was never actually achieved because her troops were defeated in the Azores. There are many scholarly commentaries on this map. The latitude crescent system instituted by Mercator in his 1569 world map influenced Guillaume Levasseur's Atlantic Ocean map of 1601 [Map 67]. Such maps were printed on parchment by the Dutch and distributed in Atlantic harbors. For the first time the name Quebec appears on a map of Canada. (Quebec was actually to be founded in 1608.)

Along the St Lawrence River there are twenty-eight other places with names that appear here for the first time. For identifying Canadian locations this may well be considered the most important map prior to Champlain's [Map 69].

The portolani of the Atlantic Ocean by Pierre de Vaulx [Map 71] include a French text and details about the new colonies in America, the ownership of each being indicated by apposite coats of arms. There is no Portuguese banner. The coast of the Gulf of Mexico is described with more detail than on previous maps.

Atlas (Oriental India and Japan), 1571. Fernão (Ferdinand) Vaz Dourado. Parchment, 54 x 40.5 cm. Instituto dos Arquivos Nacionais / Torre do Tombo, Lisbon. (Map 59)

Explorers' Lifelines

Beyond the New World: 1500-1550

Spa	Vasco de Balboa	[c.1475–1519]
Itl	Francisco Pizarro	[1475–1541]
Itl	Sebastian Cabot	[c.1476–1557]
Por	Ferdinand Magellan	[1480–1521]
Por	Antonio Pigafetta	[c.1480–c.1534]
Spa	Hernán Cortés	[1485–1547]
Itl	Giovanni da Verrazano	[c.1485–c.1528]
Por	Juan Rodriquez Cabrillo	[?–c.1543]
Spa	Pedro de Mendoza	[c.1487–1537]
Spa	Alvar Nuñez Cabeza de Vaca	[c.1490–c.1560]
Fra	Jacques Cartier	[1491–1557]
Spa	Hernando de Soto	[c.1499–1542]
Spa	Gonzalo Pizarro	[c.1502–1548]
Fra	Jean Ribaut	[c.1520–1565]
Eng	Martin Frobisher	[1535–1594]
Eng	Humphrey Gilbert	[c.1537–1583]
Eng	Francis Drake	[c.1540–1596]
Hol	Willem Barents	[c.1550–1597]
Eng	John Davis	[c.1550–1605]

Brazil, 1579.
Jacques de Vau de Claye.
Parchment, 59 x 45 cm.
Bibliothèque nationale de France,
Paris. (Map 60)

CHAPTER IV

BRIDGING THE OCEANS: 1550 – 1600

Francis Drake

To appreciate why the privateer Francis Drake is acknowledged to be the most important British seaman and explorer of the Elizabethan age, we need to distinguish between buccaneers, corsairs, pirates and privateers. They were all numerous in the second half of the seventeenth century and especially along coastal waters.

Buccaneers were pirates and privateers. Corsairs were pirates or privateers who operated in the Mediterranean, specifically along the North African coast. The commander, a crew-member or even their armed ship could be called a privateer if it/they had a commission from a bona fide government to capture merchant vessels of an enemy nation.[25]

A pirate also robs and plunders on the high seas, but does so illegally without such a commission. Of course, highly disputed applications of these distinctions often arose. For example, Francis Drake's raids and plundering of Spanish ships when England and Spain were not at war were considered by Spain to be acts of piracy.

Drake learned his trade from his elder cousin, the privateer John Hawkins. Drake commanded one of the vessels on Hawkins' third expedition along the African coast and in the Caribbean as they obtained slaves. Drake also assisted in Hawkins' capture of a Spanish fort near Veracruz.

During subsequent negotiations, however, the Spanish suddenly attacked and overpowered the British ships and crew. Two British men were executed and others were lashed then sentenced to eight years as galley slaves. Slave labor was needed for several tasks, including continually removing bilge water from the ships.

Rio de Janeiro Bay, 1579.
Jacques de Vau de Claye.
Parchment, 31 x 67 cm.
Bibliothèque nationale
de France, Paris. (Map 61)

Portuguese Map of the World (Cyprus), c. 1585.
Unknown artist.
Parchment, 114.5 x 218 cm.
Bibliothèque nationale
de France, Paris. (Map 63)

As privateers sailed the coastlines seeking their enemy, they recorded valuable data for their own and future portolani to be used by future English seamen. Drake also documented his voyage around the world.

Thomas Jefferson (1743–1826), a founding father of the United States and third President, stated that 'every possible encouragement should be given to privateering in time of war with a commercial nation'. In a Congressional order signed by John Hancock, privateers were told, 'You may, by force of arms, attack, subdue and take all ships and other vessels belonging to the Inhabitants of Great Britain.'

Cast Silver Plaque Depicting the Voyage of Sir Francis Drake, London, 1589.
Michael Mercator.
Silver, 6.9 cm.
The British Museum, London.

Atlas (South America), 1583.
Joan Martines.
Parchment, 49.5 x 59 cm.
Bibliothèque nationale de France, Paris. (Map 62)

Because the captured property of such conquests was typically divided between members of the crew, no advice was acted upon more enthusiastically by the entrepreneurs of the day. During the Revolutionary War at least 1,000 British cargo ships were captured by privateers who were sanctioned by Congress.

The naval historian Edgar Maclay noted that British newspapers during what they called the 'American War' said little of the war on land, but complained bitterly instead about US privateers that had encroached right up into the English Channel and Irish Sea.[26]

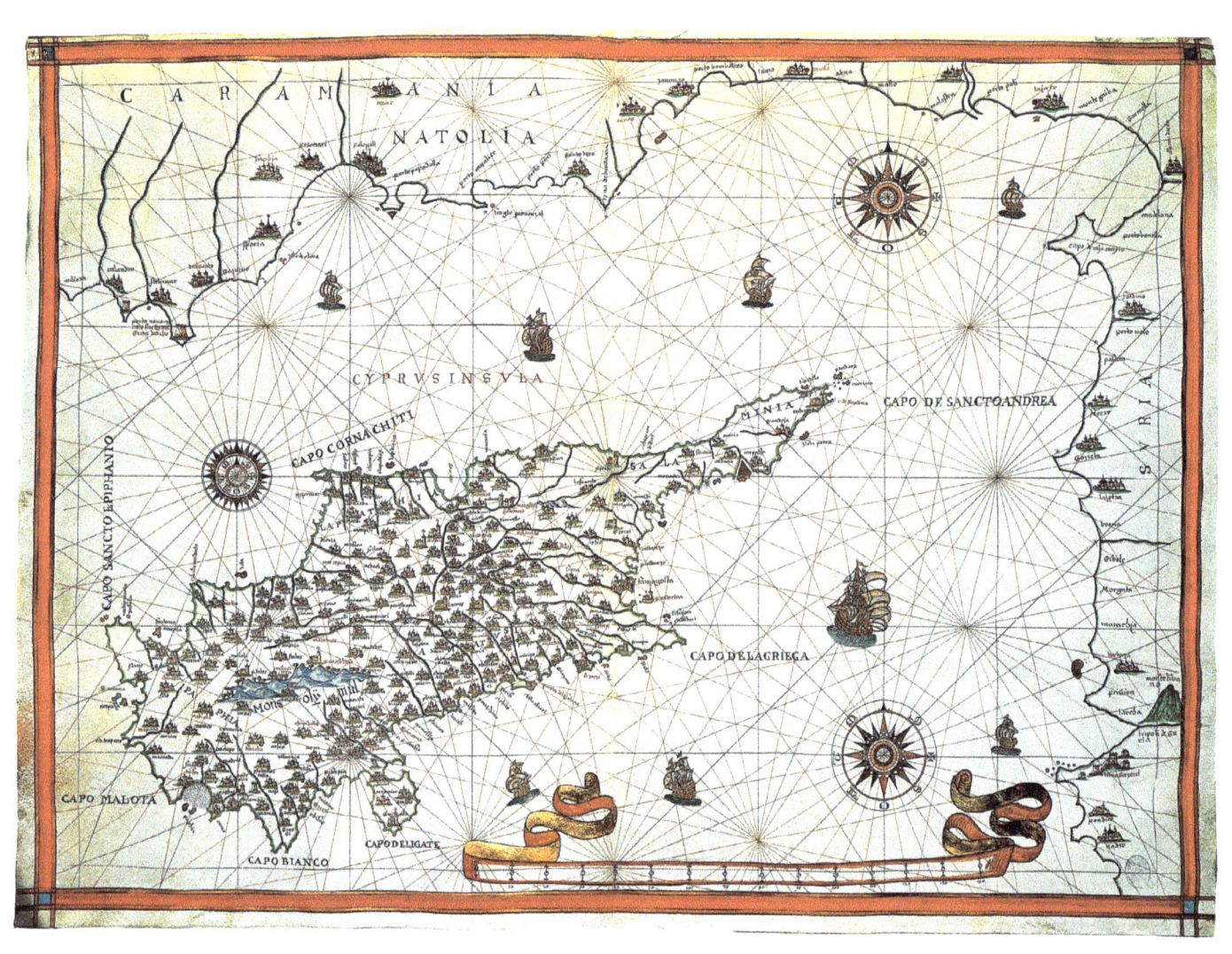

Atlas (Cyprus Isle), 1587.
Joan Martines.
Parchment, 58 x 80 cm.
Biblioteca Nacional de España,
Madrid. (Map 64)

Atlas (South East Asia), 1587.
Joan Martines.
Parchment, 58 x 80 cm.
Biblioteca Nacional de España,
Madrid. (Map 65)

QVADRIPARTITA CLASSIS OF
BRVTIORV LEGIT O CARD
VIII CRIREMIB EXPLOF
PRE

Drake's Voyage Around the World

In 1577, at the outset of that historic three-year journey, Drake's crews were not aware of their ambitious goal to circumnavigate the globe. They were therefore astonished when they sailed past Gibraltar and the route to Egypt, which they had believed to be their destination. Drake persevered, commanding his crew to sail across the Atlantic to Brazil, and by so doing became the first Englishman to sail through the Strait of Magellan.

After passing through the strait, and instead of sailing directly north-east to the Philippines as Magellan had done about sixty years earlier, Drake sailed northward along the Pacific coast. Along the way, he sacked Valparaiso in Chile and captured a Spanish treasure ship.

He then sailed for two months across the Pacific before landing in the Philippines, where he bartered with friendly natives, some acting as navigational guides through the archipelago. He documented his sightings and provided very valuable information for future Europeans to visit the area.

He sailed west across the Indian Ocean, swung in a wide loop around the southernmost point of Africa (Cape Agulhas) and turned north to return to Plymouth. There, he was immediately greeted as a national hero.

A few months after his return to Plymouth, Drake was knighted. In 1588, Sir Francis Drake then participated in the defeat of the Spanish Armada. Some eight years later, in the final year of his life, Drake's attacks on Puerto Rico and Panama both failed. He died at sea in 1596.

MARTIN FROBISHER

Martin Frobisher commanded one of the ships in Drake's 1585 expedition to the West Indies. He was also with Drake and Hawkins three years later for the defeat of the Spanish Armada.

Earlier, and for much of his youth, Frobisher had been used to undertaking voyages to and from Africa. Searching for the North-west Passage during the years 1576–78, he made three voyages to the Arctic regions, each licensed by Elizabeth I.

On his first he discovered the bay later named for him. Thinking he had reached Cathay, he brought back an Eskimo and a metallic mineral he mistakenly believed was gold.

The Battle of Lepanto,
7 October 1571.
Luca Cambiaso (1527-1585).
Oil on canvas.
Monasterio de El Escorial,
San Lorenzo de El Escorial

Atlantic Ocean, 1601.
Guillaume Levasseur.
Parchment, 74.4 x 99 cm.
Bibliothèque nationale
de France, Paris. (Map 67)

Martin Frobisher, 1570's.
Cornelius Ketel.
Bodleian Library, Oxford.

Like Drake, he was wounded while fighting the Spanish. Also like Drake, Frobisher, in spite of failures, was knighted for his bravery in those campaigns against the Spanish. He died of his wounds.

Samuel De Champlain

If there was one founder of New France or the future Canada, it was the French explorer Samuel de Champlain. In 1605, along with Pierre du Guast, Lord de Monts (1560-1611), he founded the first European settlement, later to become Montreal. However, Frobisher, La Pérouse, and de Champlain were certainly not the first Europeans to reach that part of the world.

About seventy years earlier the Frenchman Cartier, as we saw above, had first landed on the eastern extremity of the Gaspé Peninsula. Before him John Cabot had reached the same shores for England in 1497. Yet these and a small number of other Europeans who visited Canada several times during these years were merely the followers of the original Vikings who had landed there in about 1000.

Before founding Quebec, Champlain led pioneering trips up the St Lawrence and other rivers, reaching Lake Huron and Lake Ontario and finally discovered the lake that bears his name. At that particular time he was accompanied by a war party of the Algonquins and Hurons, actively supporting their eventual victory over the Iroquois near the present Ticonderoga.

Although Hollywood would later disregard the fact, the first use of firearms against the Iroquois dates to Champlain's 1609 backing for his Algonquin allies. At Ticonderoga several battles of the Franco-Indian war were later to take place, as indeed were other significant events in early US history. The siding of the Iroquois with the British dates back to Champlain's support for the nations of their enemies.

Before returning to France he commissioned others to carry on, including Jean Nicolet (who crossed Lake Huron and Lake Wisconsin) and Etienne Brulé, who sailed the Susquenhanna River down to Chesapeake Bay. Today it is difficult to appreciate the fact that these seventeenth-century explorers were envisioning a link through these rivers of New France to China. While it may seem comical to us nearly 400 years later, Peter Whitfield reminds us of the story of Nicolet, who so expected to be greeted by people of Asia, that he 'donned Chinese robes when he landed on the western shore of Lake Michigan.'[27]

Mediterranean Sea,
c. 1600-1610.
Nicolaos Vourdopolos.
Parchment, 50.5 x 59 cm.
Bibliothèque nationale
de France, Paris. (Map 66)

Atlantic Ocean,
Mediterranean Sea and
Black Sea, 1603.
Francesco Oliva.
Parchment, 54 x 90 cm.
Bibliothèque nationale
de France, Paris. (Map 68)

North Eastern Atlantic Ocean,
Mediterranean Sea and
Eastern Black Sea, c. 1610.
Harmen and Marten Jansz.
Parchment, 85 x 71 cm.
Bibliothèque nationale
de France, Paris. (Map 70)

Map of Japan from the Indian Ocean,
c. 1613. Unknown artist.
Parchment, 96.5 x 63 cm.
National Museum, Tokyo. (Map 72)

Description of New France, 1607.
Samuel de Champlain.
Parchment, 37 x 54.5 cm.
The Library of Congress, Washington, D.C.
(Map 69)

Atlantic Ocean, 1613.
Pierre de Vaulx.
Parchment, 68.1 x 95.8 cm.
Bibliothèque nationale de France,
Paris. (Map 71)

Portolani During This Period

The Breton School

Examples of portolani of the Breton school (1543-1650) centered at Le Conquet, include Maps 42-44. These show the influence of the Portugese School at Lisbon.

A pilot's practical and simple pocket guide filled with useful charts and maps was made in 1548 by Guillaume Brouscon [Map 43-44]. It tells amateur sailors how to take basic astronomical measurements for navigation, and includes a perpetual calendar and drawings of boats. A large map was folded into the volume. It presents the Atlantic coasts and the islands of the Baltic Sea, and the flags of eleven different nations, a French dictionary and the scale for calculating latitude. Several different editions of this guide exist, for it was a significant contribution to the navigation of the North Atlantic and adjacent oceans.

The Later Genovese School

Map 56 is of the Genovese school (up till 1588). Like the earlier works in this school, it was influenced by *The Pisana* [Map 1] of the thirteenth-century. Works of this school influenced the Viennese, Portugese, Spanish and Italian schools.

Map 69, the first cartographic work of de Champlain – the portolano of 1607 – shows the direct influence of the Dutch and Portugese schools. It influenced the Spanish and Breton schools. It is a description primarily of the coasts of New France and New England. To fully appreciate the work it should be studied along with his book *Les Voyages du Sieur de Champlain, Saintongeois* (1603), and his diary documenting his journey in Arcadia from 1604 to 1607. His map represents a new approach to geographical documentation based only on first-hand observation.

The Greek School

Maps 57 and 66 of the Greek school (1537-1620), centered on Crete, show the influence of the fifteenth-century Venetian school but are thought probably not to have influenced subsequent schools.

Atlas of the Mediterranean, 1620.
Charlat Ambrosin.
Parchment, 47 x 67 cm.
Bibliothèque nationale
de France, Paris. (Map 74)

Atlantic Ocean, 1618.
Domingos Sanchez.
Parchment, 95 x 84 cm.
Bibliothèque nationale
de France, Paris. (Map 73)

Aegean Sea, 1624.
Alvise Gramolin.
Parchment, 107 x 65 cm.
Bibliothèque nationale
de France, Paris. (Map 76)

*Nautical Guide to France
(Description hydrographique
de la France)*, 1628.
Jean Guérard. Parchment
stuck onto one parchment
sheet, 120.5 x 81 cm.
Bibliothèque nationale
de France, Paris. (Map 78)

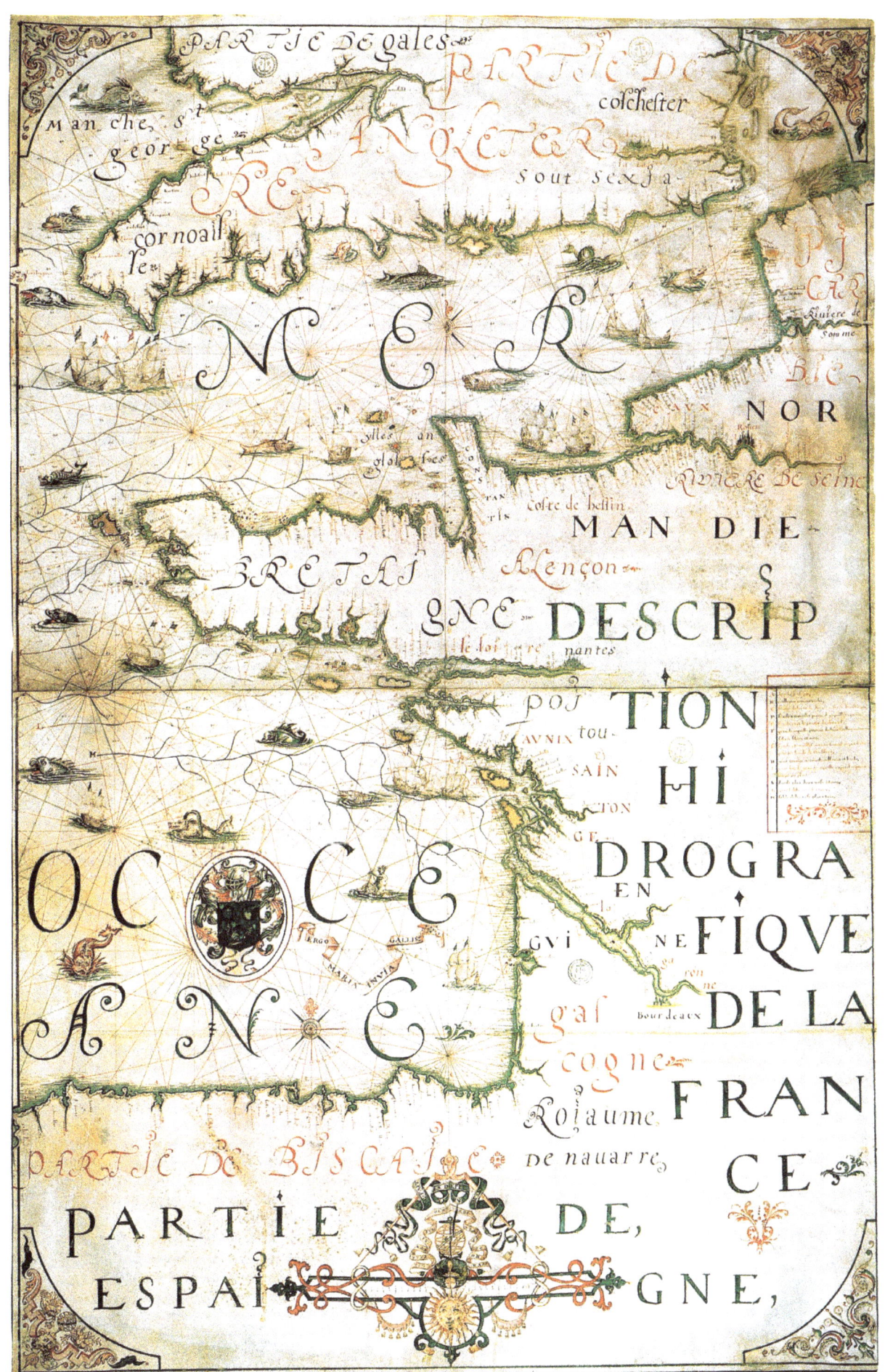

The Japanese Archipelago, 1625.
Unknown artist.
Parchment, 91.5 x 69 cm.
National Museum, Tokyo. (Map 77)

Pacific Ocean, 1622.
Hessel Gerritsz.
Parchment, 107 x 141 cm.
Bibliothèque nationale de France, Paris. (Map 75)

Explorers' Lifelines

Bridging the Oceans: 1550–1600

Eng	William Adams	[1564–1620]
Fra	Samuel de Champlain	[c.1567–c.1635]
Eng	Henry Hudson	[c.1550–1611]
Eng	William Baffin	[c.1584–1622]
Fra	Etienne Brulé	[c.1592–c.1632]
Fra	Jean Nicolet	[c.1598–1642]

North Atlantic Ocean, c. 1628.
Hessel Gerritsz.
Parchment, 112 x 87 cm.
Bibliothèque nationale de France,
Paris. (Map 79)

CHAPTER V

THE RENAISSANCE OF DISCOVERY: 1600 – 1700

HENRY HUDSON

Englishman Henry Hudson's voyage of 1610-11 continued the search for a North-west Passage to the Pacific Ocean that fellow-countryman John Davis had endeavored to find over twenty years before. Before them, we saw that explorers Frobisher and Cartier also tried, all three during the sixteenth century.

Davis went the furthest north, into the strait now named for him, whereas Hudson went the furthest west, into the vast bay he soon realised was not the Pacific. His fourth voyage traveled beyond Davis' own exploration up Davis Strait.

Both English and Dutch claims to North American lands were advanced by the explorations of Hudson. An English company paid for his first voyage, but his second was for the Dutch East India Company. Dutch claims on the territory would include the area that became New Amsterdam, then New York City. It began with Hudson's second voyage, when he sailed up the river that would eventually be named for him to the area of present-day Albany.

The portolano that Hudson used actually already indicated the strait, bay, and river, but he would probe and document them more extensively than did the any of the European explorers who preceded him.

After many disappointments and difficulties, Hudson's crew grew discontented. That was especially true of Henry Greene, a crewman with whom Hudson had quarrelled. A mutiny led by Greene was successful. The tragic result was that Hudson and his teenaged son, along with seven members of his crew, were set adrift in a small rowboat to perish, ironically in Hudson's Bay (see p. 174).

The Northern Ocean, 1628.
Jean Guérard.
Parchment stuck onto one parchment sheet,
86 x 128 cm.
Bibliothèque nationale de France, Paris. (Map 80)

Atlas, c. 1630.
Unknown artist.
Parchment, 27 x 38 cm.
Bibliothèque nationale de France, Paris. (Map 81)

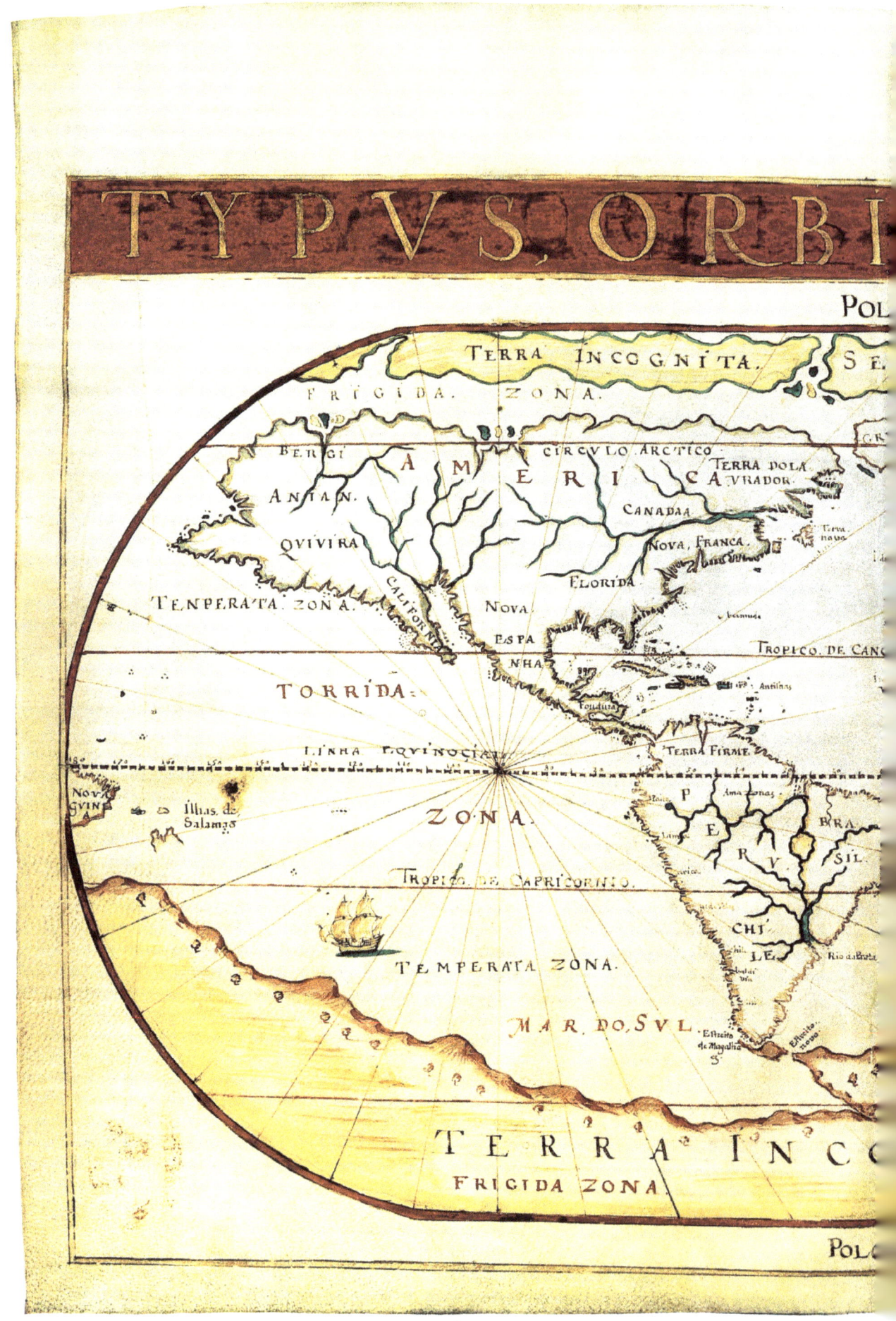

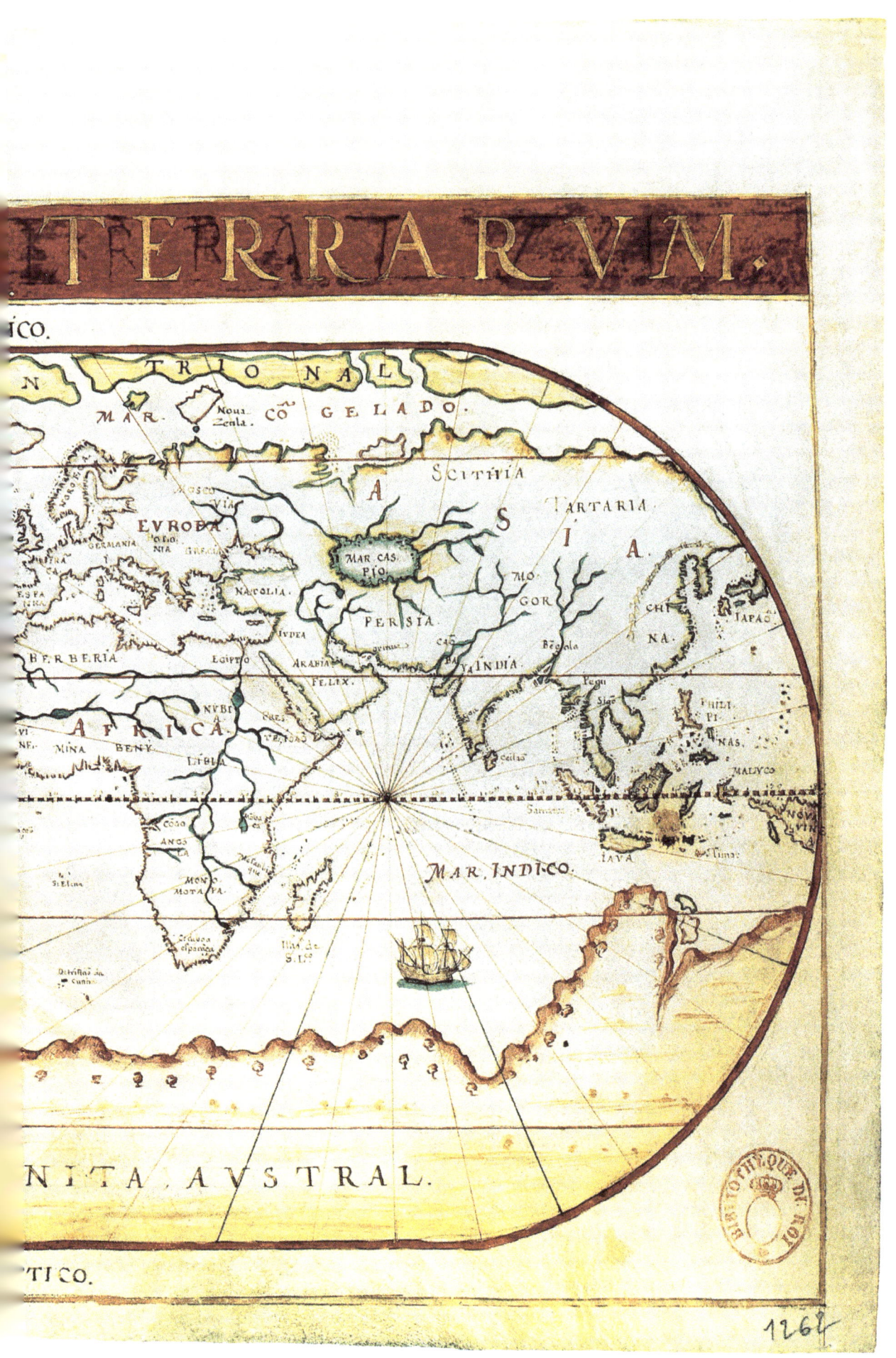

There is no evidence that anyone survived. It was an inglorious end to a life of heroic exploration that lacked the religious extremes, greed or yearning for personal glory that many, if not most, other contemporary explorers exhibited.

For the return to England, Robert Bylot was elected the leader of the mutinous crew. But along the way Eskimos killed Greene and several others, and more died of starvation. The few who finally reached England were imprisoned.

The Last Voyage of Henry Hudson, 1881. The Hon. John Collier (1850-1934). Oil on canvas, 214 x 183.5 cm. Tate Britain, London.

ABEL JANSZOON TASMAN

The greatest of Dutch navigators, Abel Janszoon Tasman, is most obviously associated with the discovery of the island now named Tasmania (see p. 175). However, Tasman is less recognised for his other achievements that are just as great:

the discovery of New Zealand, and Tonga, and the islands of Fiji. Tasman was also the first European to circumnavigate Australia. Several of his countrymen had already explored portions of the north and west coasts of 'the Southern Land' (*Terra Australis*), but Tasman proved that it was a vast continental island. In doing so, he also took soundings (to document the water's depth) around the entire coast of Australia.

Tasman's contribution to mapping is momentous. He was the first to map the coastline of the Gulf of Carpentaria, which perhaps he also named. Earlier he had named the bay eventually called Cook's Strait – he called it Moordenaars (Murderers), although that was later translated to Massacre Bay, because natives killed several of Tasman's crew there.

Back in his homeland, Tasman held several important administrative posts, and was personally involved in the declaration of a truce between the Dutch East India Company and the Portuguese in India. However, his final years included more nautical exploration, such as his command of a commercial trade fleet to Siam (present-day Thailand) and later his leadership of a warfleet to fight the Spaniards in the Philippines.

PORTOLANI DURING THIS PERIOD

The early seventeenth-century explorers of the New World including de Champlain, Hudson, and Baffin, and the explorers of the Pacific including Tasman, created and had available to them maps [similar to Maps 44–65] that were beginning to look like our own present-day ones.

Explorers of the seventeenth century including Marquette and Dampier could have known of maps [such as Maps 66–94] that included a considerable quantity of authenticated data, reflecting the centuries of navigation prior to them.

The Marseille School

Maps 74, 83, 89 are of the Marseille school (1590–1672). They show the marked influence of the school at Messina (1537–1620) and in turn influenced the Paris school (1661–1751).

Five parchment sheets were used in 1620 by Charlat Ambrosin for his map of the Mediterranean [Map 74]. It introduced inset maps-within-the-map, showing three details, each with a different compass orientation: Malta (in the lower right),

Portrait of Abel Tasman, his Wife and Daughter, 1637. Jacob Gerritsz Cuyp (1594–c.1651). Oil on canvas, 106.7 × 132.1 cm. National Library of Australia, Canberra.

175

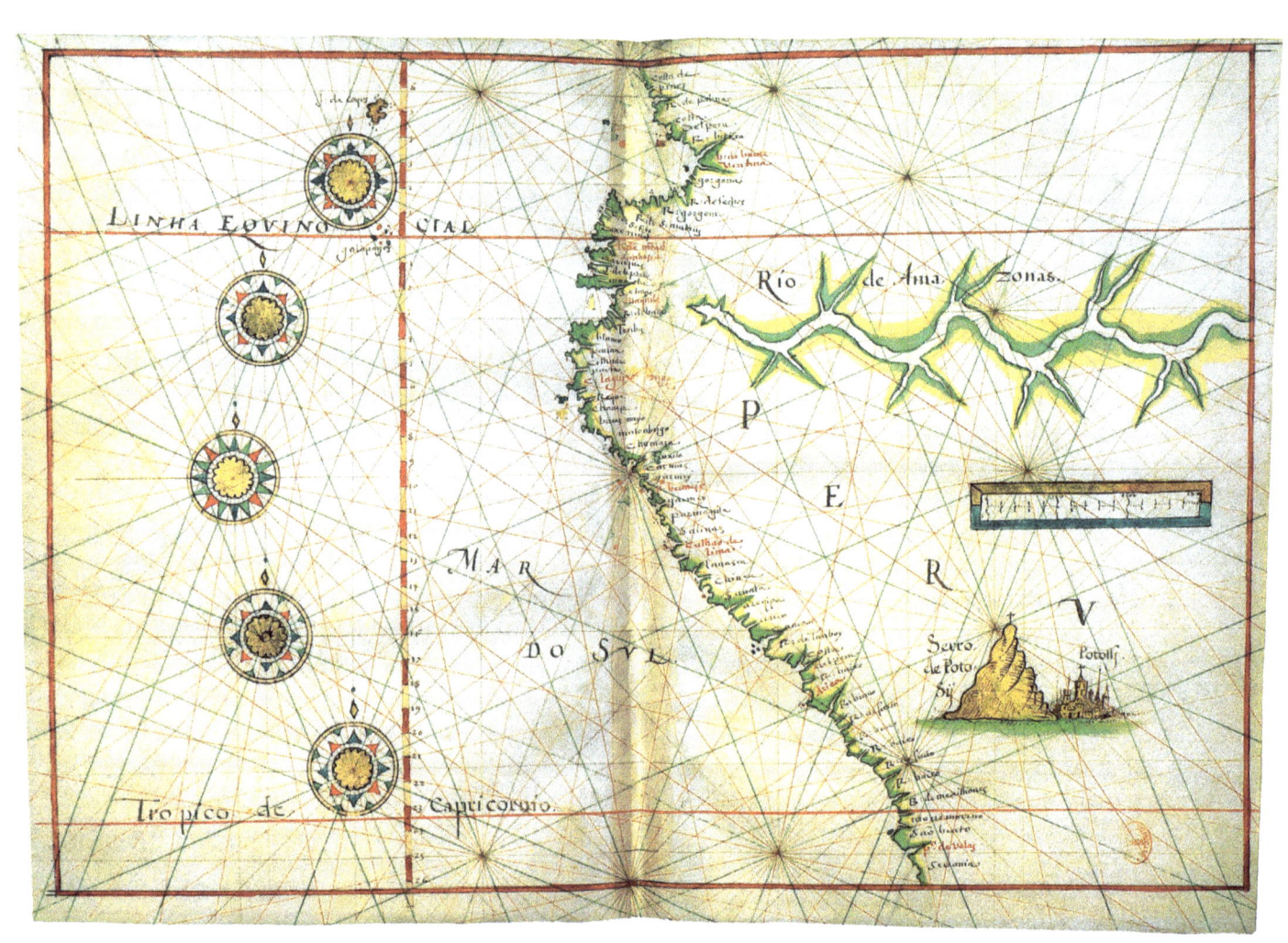

Atlas (Peru Coasts), c. 1630.
Unknown artist.
Parchment, 27 x 38 cm.
Bibliothèque nationale de France, Paris.
(Map 82)

Provençal Atlas of the Mediterranean, 1633.
Augustin Roussin.
Parchment, 27.7 x 39.4 cm.
(Map 83)

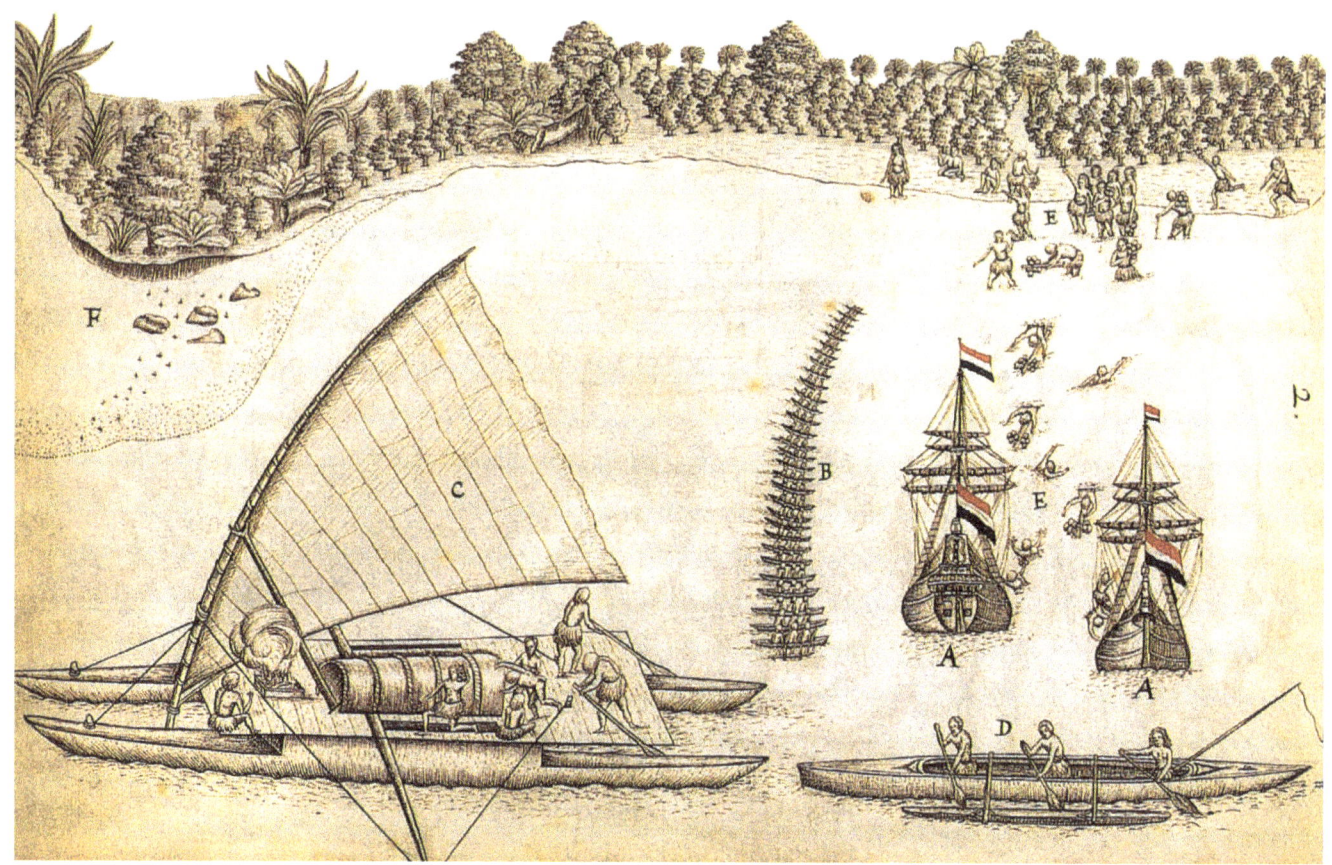

Sicily and the North African coast. Interiors, such as that of Tunis, are exceptionally detailed for the time.

The Japanese School

The portolani of the Japanese school centered in Nagasaki (1592–1636) show the influence of only the Portuguese school. See, for example, the anonymous maps of Japan viewed from the Indian Ocean [Map 72, c. 1613], or from the archipelago [Map 77, of 1625]. The first Portuguese journey to Japan was in 1541–1543. It was the beginning of an important commercial relationship between the two countries. During the next forty-seven years (1543-1590) eighty ships arrrived in Japan from Portugal.

Tasman's Ship in Tonga.
Extract from Tasman's journals.
National State Archive,
The Hague.

Indian Ocean, 1634.
João Teixeira Albernas.
Parchment, 84.5 x 70.5 cm.
Bibliothèque nationale
de France, Paris. (Map 85)

The Viennese School

Map 76 is of the Viennese school (1367–1690). Along with earlier examples from this school [Maps 10, 11, 15, 18, 19] it shows the influence of the Genovese school. Earlier examples influenced the Spanish and Turkish schools.

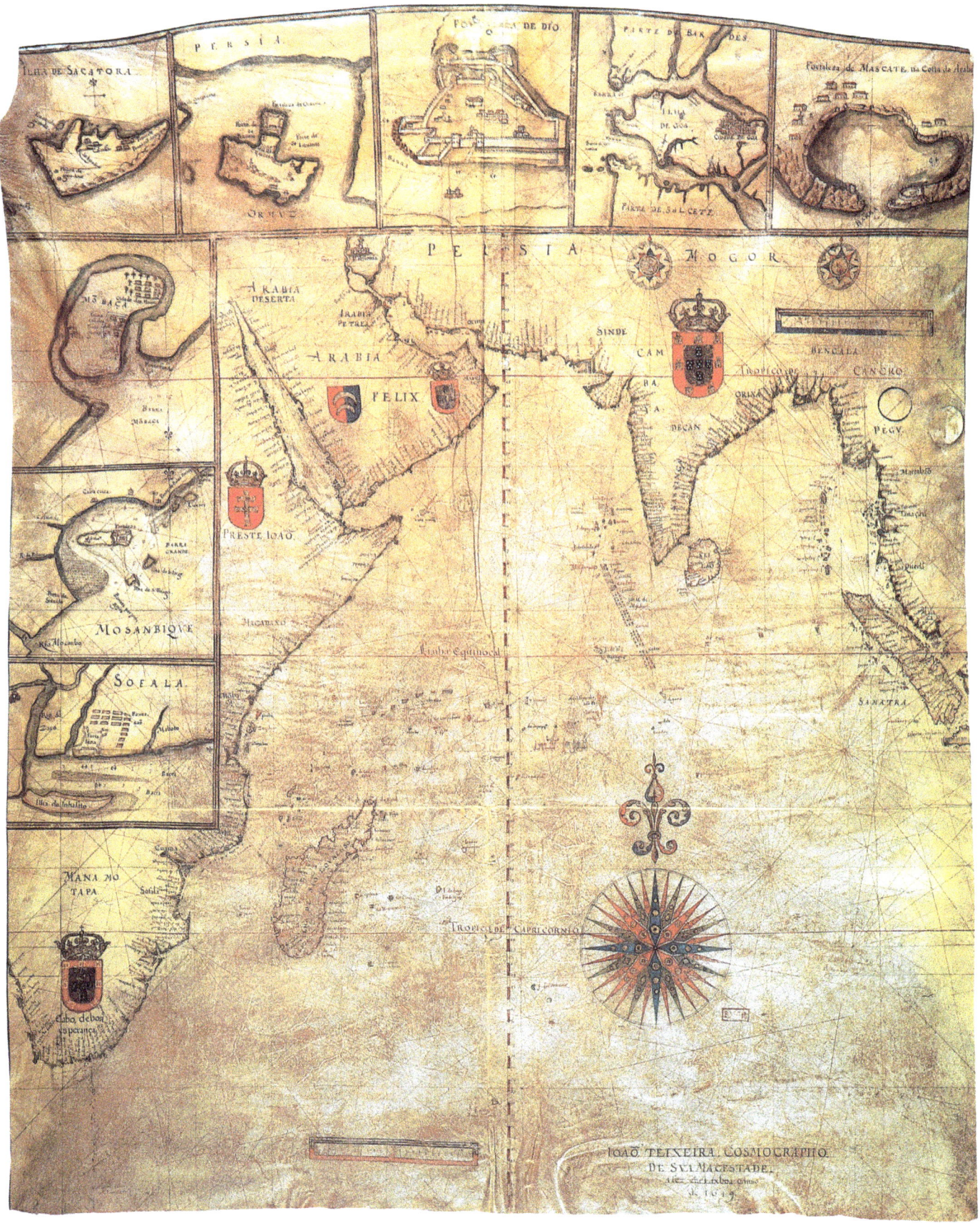

Nautical World Map, 1634.
Jean Guérard.
Parchment, 39.6 x 47.9 cm.
Bibliothèque nationale de France, Paris.
(Map 84)

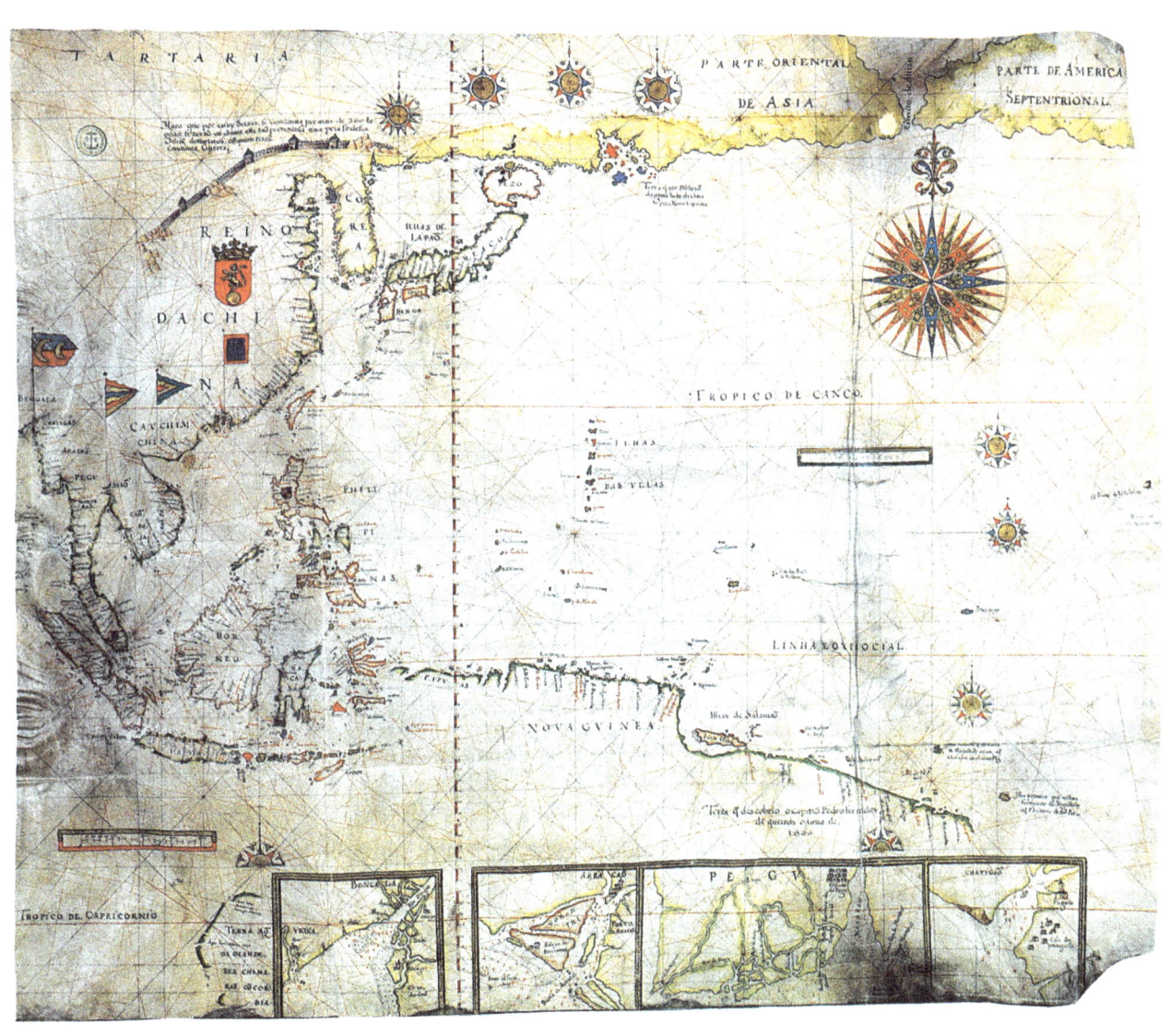

Pacific Ocean, 1649.
João Teixeira Albernas.
Parchment, 89 x 74 cm.
Bibliothèque nationale de France, Paris.
(Map 86)

Indian Ocean, 1660.
Pieter Goos.
Parchment, 71.5 x 89 cm.
Bibliothèque nationale de France, Paris.
(Map 87)

The Madagascar Roadstead, 1660.
Fred Woldemar.
Parchment, 70.5 x 90 cm.
Bibliothèque nationale de France, Paris.
(Map 88)

The Basque School

Maps 91 and 97 of the Basque school (1579–1690), centered at Saint Jean de Luz, show the influence of the fifteenth-century school at La Rochelle (1493–1559).

The map of the North Atlantic [Map 91] by Denis de Rotis in 1674 reflects Basque-French commercial activity during the seventeenth century. They had thirty-nine whaling ships and twenty trawlers, monopolising the whaling industry until the end of the eighteenth century. Note Labrador at the top of the map and the 'North-west Passage' (Hudson's Bay) clearly indicated north of Canada. The other map of the Basque school [Map 97], drawn up fifteen years after the de Rotis map, represents the coasts frequented most by the Basques.

The Late English School

English school Maps 90, 93, 95, 98, 99, and 100 of the late sixteenth century show the influence of the Spanish (1508–1709) and Normandy (1536–1635) schools.

Mediterranean Sea, 1662.
François Ollive.
Parchment stuck onto one parchment sheet,
68 x 97.5 cm.
Bibliothèque nationale de France, Paris. (Map 89)

Indian Ocean, 1665.
John Burston.
Parchment, 78 x 94.5 cm.
Bibliothèque nationale de France, Paris. (Map 90)

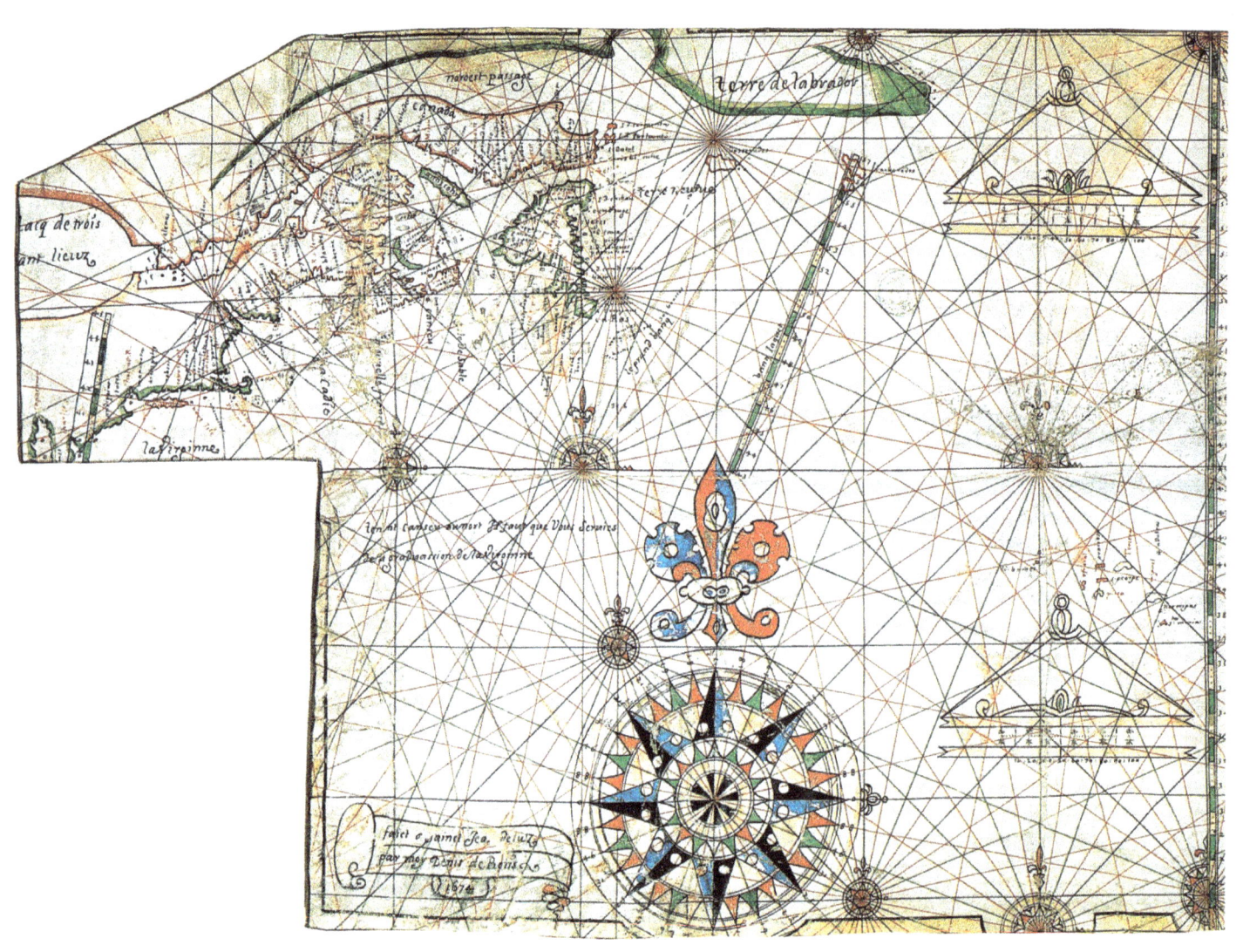

North Atlantic Ocean, 1674.
Denis de Rotis.
Parchment, 88 x 43.5 cm.
Bibliothèque nationale de France, Paris.
(Map 91)

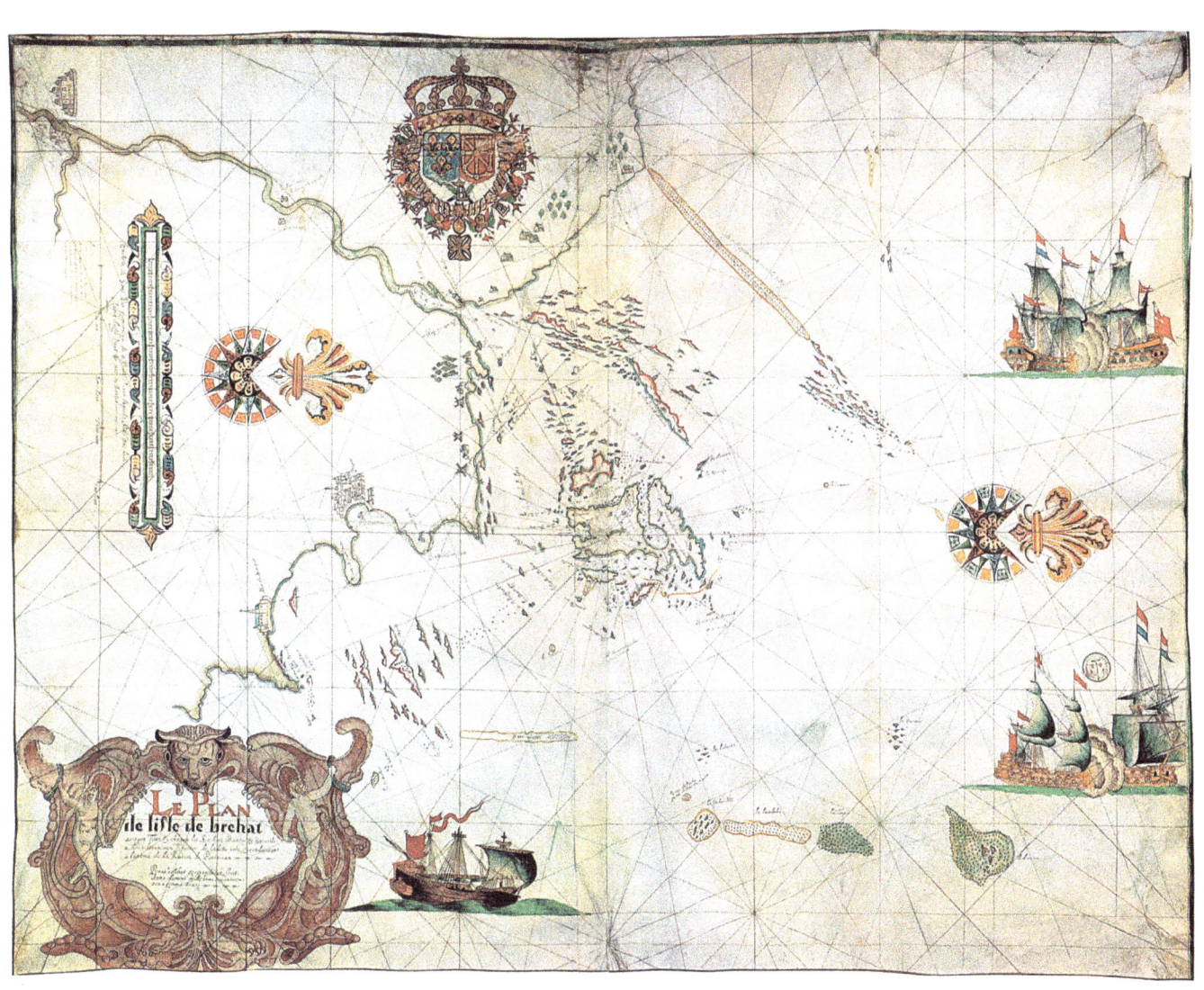

Île-de-Bréhat, 1666.
Pierre Collin.
Parchment, 96 x 75 cm.
Bibliothèque nationale de France, Paris.
(Map 92)

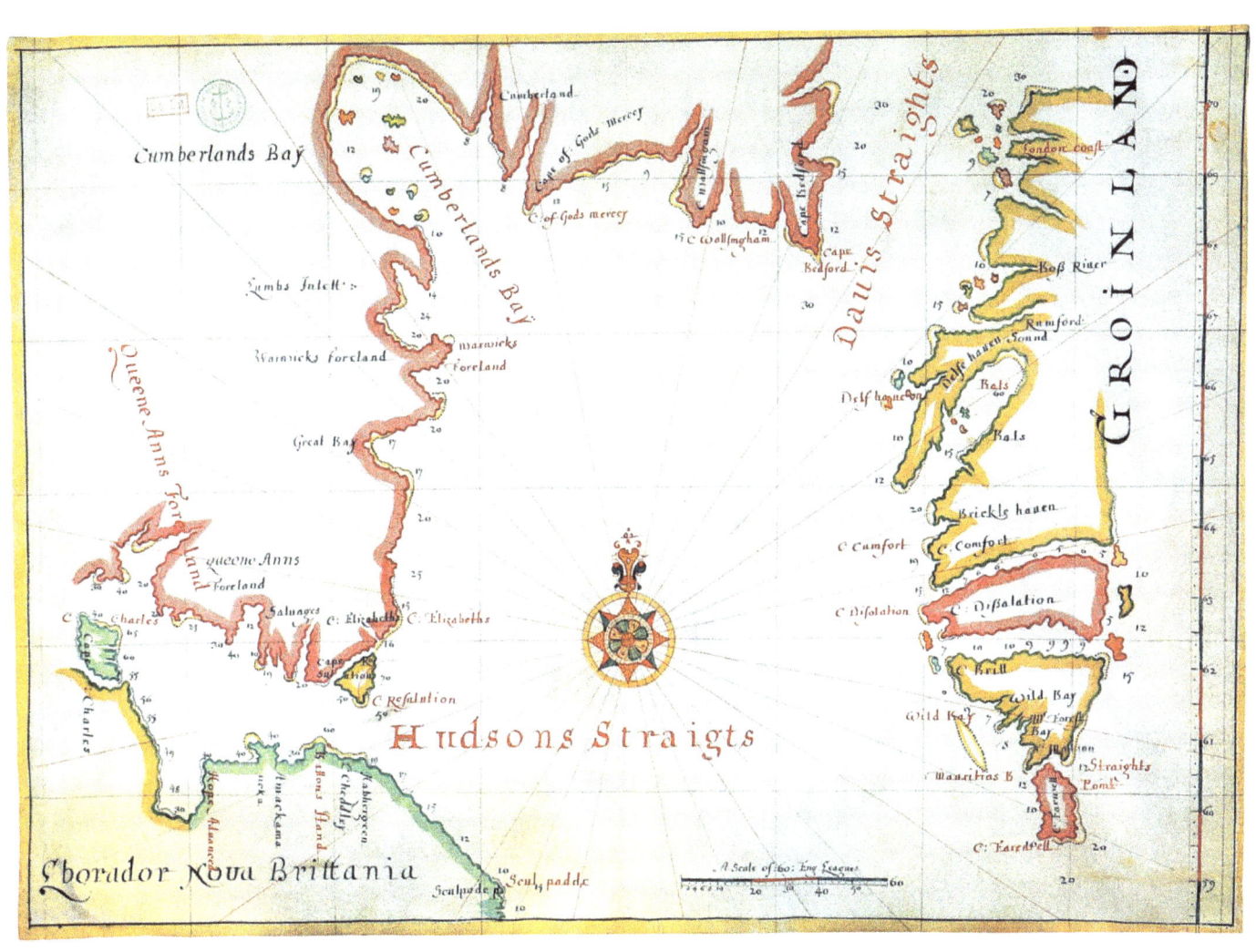

The Monomotapa Empire, 1677.
João Teixeira Albernas, the Younger.
Parchment, 61.5 x 50 cm.
Bibliothèque nationale de France, Paris.
(Map 94)

The Hudson and Davis Straits, before 1677.
Unknown artist.
Parchment, 40.6 x 57 cm.
Bibliothèque nationale de France, Paris.
(Map 93)

Mocha, 1683.
Augustine Fitzhugh.
Parchment, 32.5 x 38.5 cm.
Bibliothèque nationale de France,
Paris. (Map 95)

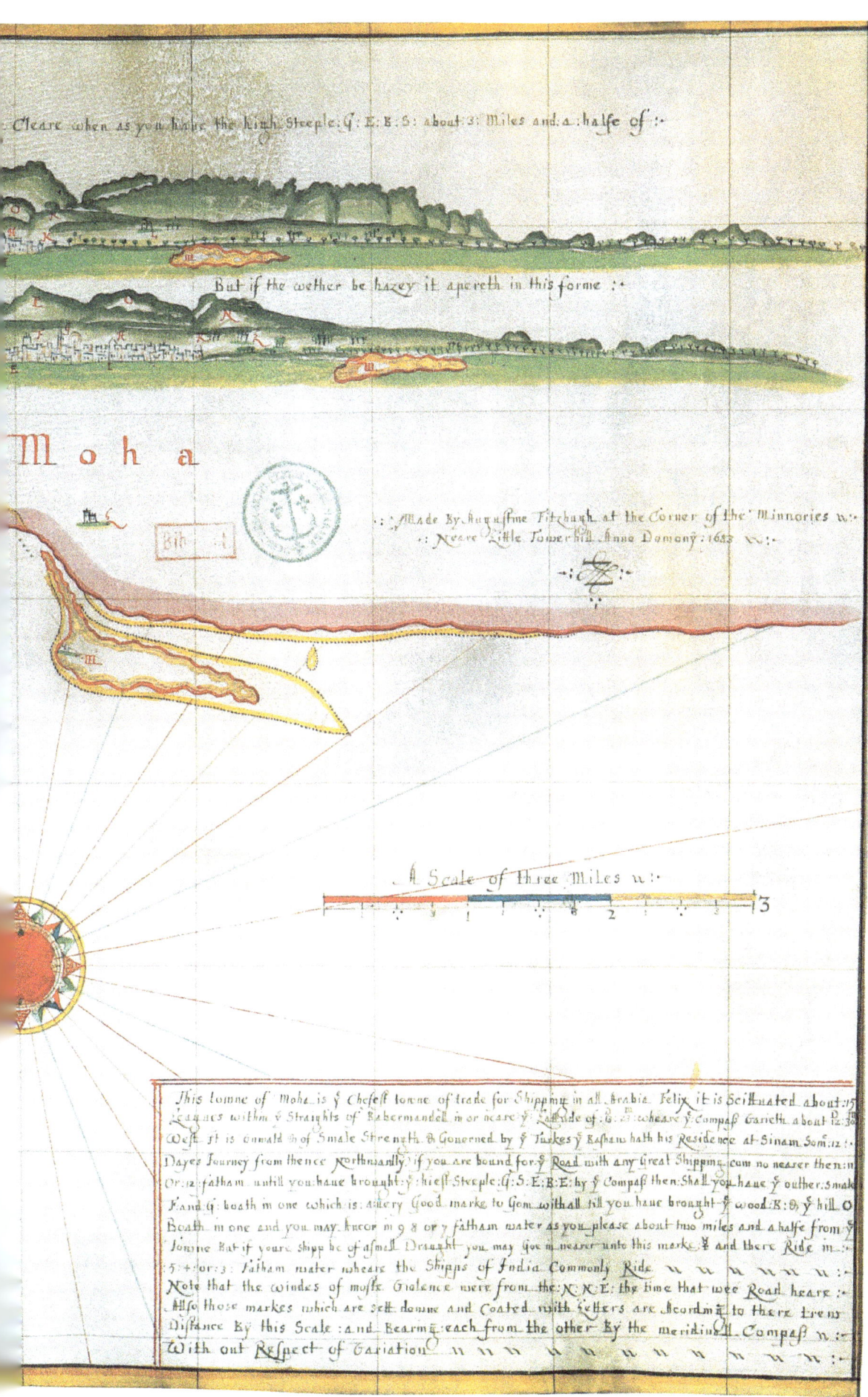

Cleare when as you haue the high Steeple G: E: B: S: about 3: Miles and a halfe of:

But if the wether be hazey it apereth in this forme:

Moha

Made By Augustine Fitzhugh at the Corner of the Minnories
Neare Little Towerhill Anno Domony 1683

A Scale of Three Miles

This towne of Moha is ye Chefest towne of trade for Shippinge in all Arabia Felix it is Scittuated about 15 leagues within ye Straights of Babermandell in or neare ye Latitude of 13: 30: wheare ye Compass Variethe about 12: 30 West it is onwald th of Smale Strenght & Governed by ye Turkes ye Bashaw hath his Residence at Sinam Som 12 Dayes Journey from thence Northnianly if you are bound for ye Road with any Great Shippinge com no neare then in Or 12 fatham untill you haue brought ye hieft Steeple G: S: E: B: E: by ye Compass then Shall you haue ye outher Smale F and G: boath in one which is a very Good marke to Com withall till you haue brought ye wood B: & ye hill O Boath in one and you may knoor in 9 8 or 7 fatham water as you please about two miles and a halfe from ye Towne But if youre shipp be of a small Draught you may Goe in neare unto this marke ¥ and there Ride in 5 4 or 3 fatham water wheare the Shipps of India Commonly Ride
Note that the windes of moste Violence were from the N: N: E: the time that wee Road heare
Allso those markes which are sett downe and Coated with letters are Acording to there trew Distance by this Scale and Bearing each from the other by the meridinall Compass with out Respect of Variation

An anonymous portolano [Map 93] dated 1675 reflects the recent explorations of Frobisher, Davis, Hudson, Button, and Baffin. However, there are many geographical mistakes in it, such as the absence of the Frobisher coast and the incorrect orientation of Labrador. Again, as elsewhere [cf. Map 91], Hudson's Bay is called 'the North-west Passage'.

The small port of Mocha (in what is now Yemen) became an important commercial center for the coffee trade during the seventeenth century. The portolano by Augustine Fitzhugh [Map 95] dated 1683 was made one year after the English market was established. There are two views: one on a bright day and the other on a cloudy day. A long text gives navigation instructions and precautions. The cartographer describes the place and access to it as if he had been on an expedition there himself.

Nutmeg and other spices come from a group of Indonesian islands called the Banda Isles [Map 98] that resulted from volcanic eruptions centuries ago. The large anonymous map indicates the routes and distances between the three principal islands of Banda, Naira and Gunape. Discovered by the Portuguese, they were controlled by the Dutch in the seventeenth century.

The last two portolani in the collection are beautiful examples of the Thames school by John Thornton, an apprentice between 1656 and 1664 of John Burston (cf. Map 90). He was the cartographer for the maps for all of the voyages of the Hudson's Bay Company and the East India Company. He produced forty-four manuscripts between 1667 and 1701, but he was famous for his atlas called *The English Pilot* that included thirty-five maritime maps published for the first time in London in 1683. The map of the Persian/Arabian Gulf [Map 99] is in Dutch and includes the discoveries of Cornelius Cornelisz Roobker in 1645. His map of Amoy Bay [Map 100] is based on original observations made by the English during voyages along the Chinese coasts.

The French School

The French school portolano [Map 92], circa 1660, benefited from being influenced by the sixteenth-century schools at Amsterdam, Dieppe, London, and Marseille. The map, dated 1666, is from the time of historic economic reconstruction in France, at the time when Jean Baptiste Colbert (1619–1683) was the finance minister to Louis XIV (from 1658 until his death). From 1668 to 1672 Colbert was particularly concerned with building up the French navy.

Map of the Island of Newfoundland, 1689. Pierre Detcheverry. Parchment, 57 x 31.5 cm. Bibliothèque nationale de France, Paris. (Map 97)

The Coast of North West Java, 1688. Joan Blaeu. Parchment, 41.5 x 103 cm. Bibliothèque nationale de France, Paris. (Map 96)

The Banda Islands, c. 1690. Unknown artist. Parchment, 35.5 x 54 cm. Bibliothèque nationale de France, Paris. (Map 98)

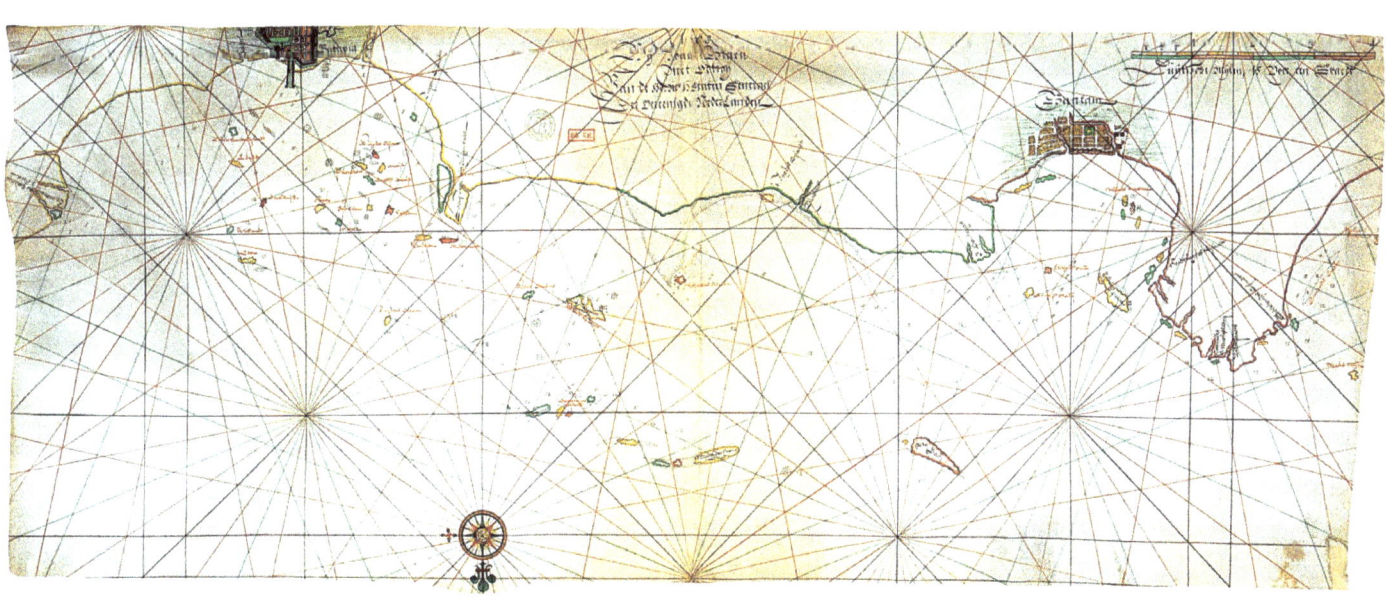

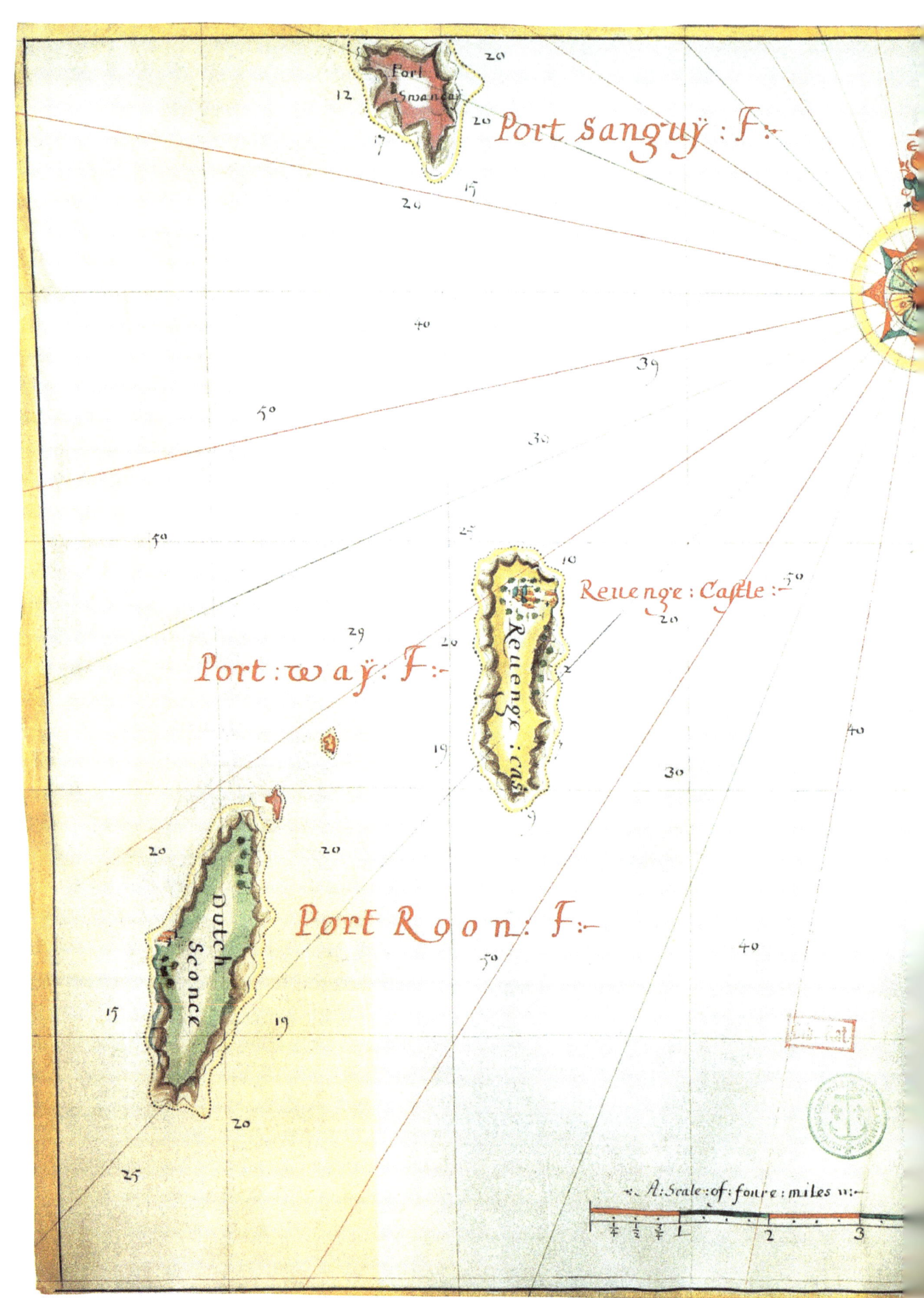

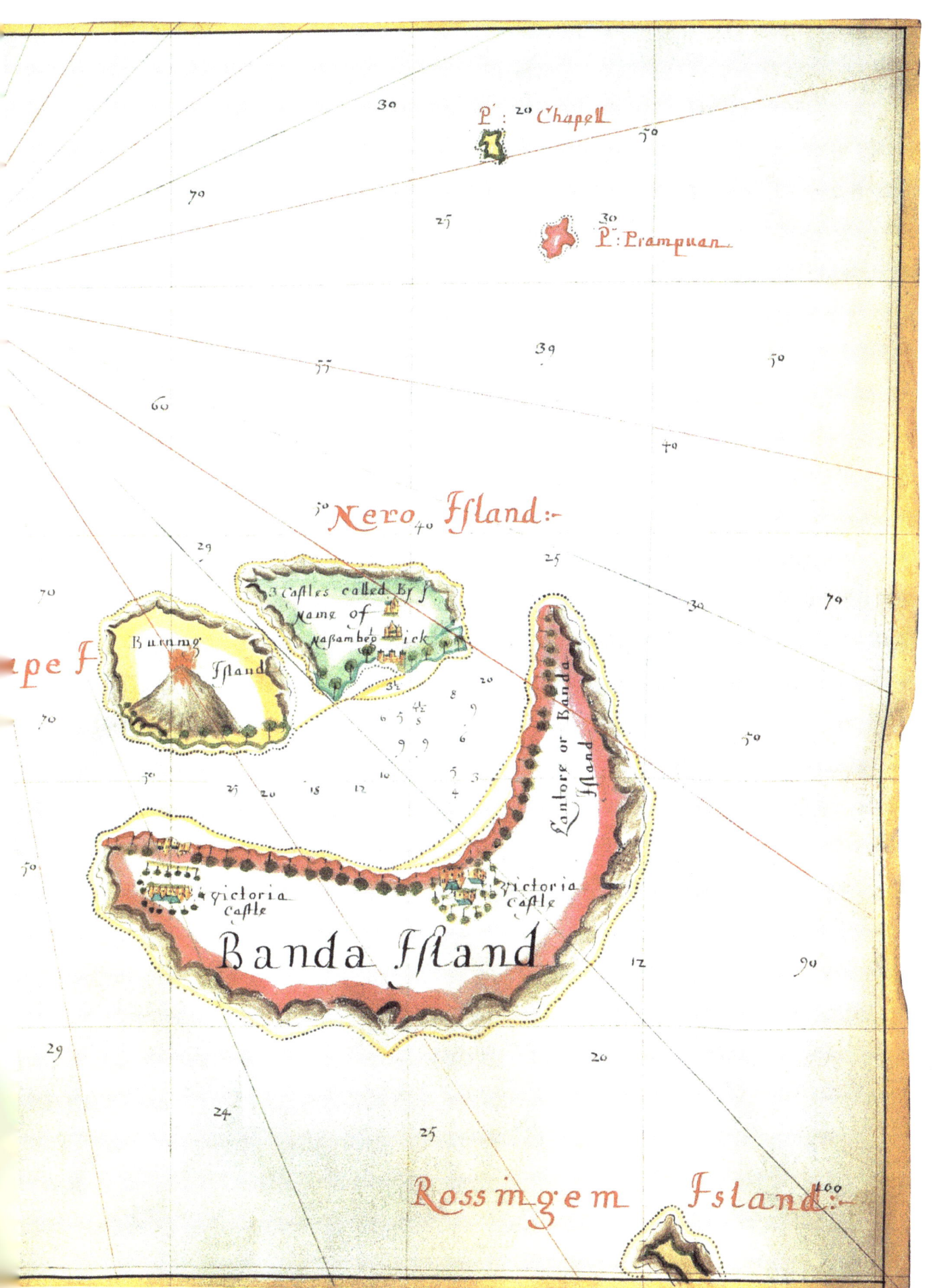

Persian/Arabian Gulf, 1699.
John Thornton.
Parchment, 63.5 x 74.5 cm.
Bibliothèque nationale de France,
Paris. (Map 99)

Amoy Bay, 1699.
John Thornton.
Parchment, 78 x 60.5 cm.
Bibliothèque nationale de France,
Paris. (Map 100)

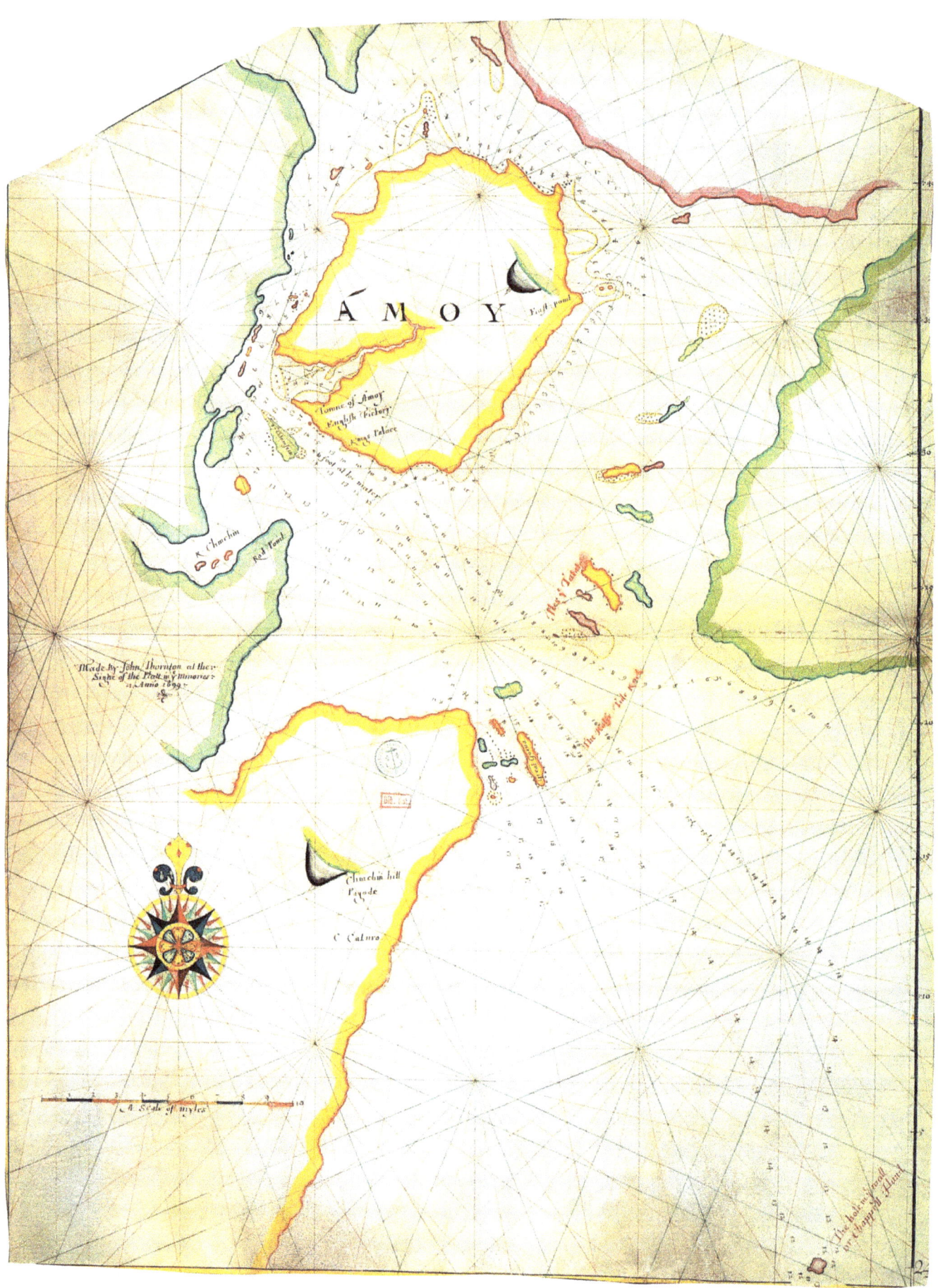

Explorers' Lifelines

The Renaissance of Discovery: 1600–1700

Eng	Henry Hudson	[1570–1611]
Hol	Abel Janszoon Tasman	[c.1603–c.1659]
Eng	Reign: Charles I of England	[1625–1649]
Fra	Pierre Esprit Radisson	[c.1636–c.1710]
Fra	Jacques Marquette	[c.1637–1675]
Hol	William Dampier	[c.1652–1715]
Fra-Can	Pierre le Moyne d'Iberville	[c.1661–1706]

CHAPTER VI

SAILING TOWARDS THE MODERN WORLD: 1700 – 1900

JAMES COOK

In the portolani drawn up before the time of Magellan, we see that European mapmakers imagined that the South Pacific was much smaller than in fact it is. Instead the cartographers envisioned a large land-mass occupying most of the area. They named it *Terra Australis Incognita* (the Unknown Southern Land) (see p. 202-203).

Even Magellan believed the land-mass on his ship's port side as he passed through the strait from the Atlantic to the Pacific was part of that fabled great southern continent. Drake was to discover that the land was actually an island (it was later named *Tierra del Fuego*).

The great English navigator James Cook (See above) would finally destroy the myth of *Terra Australis Incognita*. Before Cook's data was incorporated into such maps, portolani often gave artistic interpretations of the imagined continent.

Several explorers before Cook had shown the envisioned continent to be smaller by virtue of sailing through areas anticipated by these earlier maps to be part of this land. Cook too did this first himself, for example, on his way to Tahiti in 1769.

He was unique for his day in his more realistic estimate of the size of Antarctica, the actual southern continent.

Many of his colleagues speculated that the largest continent on Earth existed where in fact the South Pacific would prove to be. Rulers convinced of the vastness of this land were eager for their navigators to reach it and claim it for their country, for they wanted to believe it would surely be as full of riches as other discovered new lands had proved to be.[28]

Map of the New Hebrides (now called Vanuatu) and New Caledonia, in *Atlas of the World*, Rome, 1798. Sforesco Castle, Milan.

Captain James Cook, 1775-1776.
Nathaniel Dance (1735-1811).
Oil on canvas, 127 x 101.6 cm.
National Maritime Museum, Greenwich.

Complete Map of All Nations, c. 1620.
Giulio Aleni (1582-1649).

James Cook was born in 1728 – coincidentally the year Vitus Bering discovered the important passage that after him was named the Bering Strait. Fifty years later, Cook would also be drawn to that location.

Before the three great voyages for which he is most noted, Cook sailed to Canada to help survey the St Lawrence River channel. There he also fought for England against Quebec during the Seven Years' War.

After the war he remained in the area surveying the coasts of Labrador, Newfoundland, and Nova Scotia. Unlike most charts made before his time, as well as most of those published in his own day, Cook's maps were scientifically drawn up and scrupulously accurate.

One of the assignments Cook was to carry out during his first voyage around the world was to observe an exceptional astrological event: the 1769 transit of the planet Venus.

The transit was an event of global importance, for astronomers around the world were hoping to gather data. German explorer Peter Simon Pallas had traveled through Russia to the Chinese frontier to be able to observe the phenomenon.

Astronomers had determined this rare happening would best be seen from the island of Tahiti that had only recently been discovered by Samuel Wallis of England. With new data, they expected to be better able to measure the Earth's distance from the sun. This would then help in the accurate measurement of longitude and latitude, thereby permitting more precise navigation.

The Royal Society knew Cook was qualified to make such calculations. He had previously determined the longitude of Newfoundland by observing a solar eclipse in 1766. His paper on that observation greatly impressed the Society.

Cook's First Voyage

Cook's first voyage was to achieve several important goals besides documenting the life he found in these strange new lands (see previous page and aside). Not the least of these was to anticipate and successfully prevent scurvy, the serious disease that ship crews before him rarely escaped. Typically, scurvy killed up to one-third of the crew on any lengthy expedition. Cook learned that scurvy was caused by a deficiency in vitamin C. He took along citrus prod-ucts, fresh meat, and vegetables – much better provisions than had been given crews in the past. Consequently, only one of the 112 men during the three years of Cook's second voyage died of disease, and it was not from scurvy. Eventually the British routinely supplied their seamen and soldiers with sources of the needed vitamin, such as lime-juice.

The year 1642 was pivotal for science: Galileo Galilei died, Isaac Newton was born, and Abel Tasman reached New Zealand, albeit believing that he was seeing the coast of the fabled Great Southern Continent, with a bay interrupting the coast.

The next European to explore the same location was Cook, over a century later. He found that what his predecessor had thought was a continent's coastline with a bay was in fact two islands divided by a strait – now Cook's Strait. The islands would later be named New Zealand.

His assignments completed, Cook could return to England. But instead he sailed to New Holland, later to be named Australia.

He knew of Tasman's discovery of a century earlier, but map-makers still did not know if Tasmania was an island or, for example, a peninsula of Australia. Unfortunately, bad weather kept him from finding out. The question remained unanswered for at least twenty years more.

Cook went on to be the first European in over a century to pass through the Torres Strait, confirming it as a passageway between Australia and New Guinea. At Batavia in Java, malaria and dysentery claimed the lives of more than thirty of Cook's men, a tragic end to an expedition that had seen both great successes and disappointments.

Two years after the Venus transit, Cook returned to England in 1771 and gave his report to the Royal Society. However, it contributed little if anything of true scientific significance.

Also, by then armchair explorers may have grown accustomed to expecting the spectacular – happening seemingly every other day, maybe discoveries were becoming rather commonplace. After all, the year before James Bruce had

Cynoramphus Zealandicus, Black-Fronted Parakeet and *Cochlospermum Gillivraei, Kapok Tree*, Watercolours by Sydney Parkinson (c. 1745-1771) from Sir Joseph Banks' commission of natural history drawings from Captain James Cook's first voyage (*Endeavour* 1768-1771). Natural History Museum, London.

Phaethon Rubricauda, Redtailed Tropicbird. Watercolour by Sydney Parkinson (c. 1745-1771) from Sir Joseph Banks' commission of natural history drawings from Captain James Cook's first voyage (*Endeavour* 1768-1771). Natural History Museum, London.

The Sandwich Islands (Later Known as the Hawaiian Islands), in *Atlas of the World*, Rome, 1798. Sforzesco Castle, Milan.

discovered the source of the Blue Nile, and the year after Cook's report Bruce traced the Blue Nile to its confluence with the White Nile.

On the plus side, after Cook's first voyage New Zealand and Australia were now known to be islands and might be added to the British Empire. However, it was still not proven that the Great Southern Continent existed.

So a second around-the-world voyage was commissioned, with hopes that the southern latitudes would be fully explored.

Cook's Second Voyage

In 1772, on Cook's second voyage, the men in his fleet were the first on record to cross the Antarctic Circle. They pressed on as far as they could through the ice, but there was still no sighting of the Great Southern Continent. The men spent the winter in New Zealand and revisited Tahiti, charting nearby islands that Cook named the Friendly Islands (see p. 221) because of the warm reception he received from the natives.

One of the two ships in the expedition, damaged by storms, was forced to return to England, becoming the first ship to circumnavigate the world from west to east.

Meanwhile, Cook took the other ship into the Antarctic Circle for the second time. He proceeded further south than anyone had ever gone or would go again for nearly fifty years. He declared that 'no continent is to be found in this ocean.'

Supplies and the crew's strength were both low. Shortly after the Antarctic probe, the ship's physician said that Cook, sick with 'bilious colic', needed fresh meat. There was apparently at most only salted meat on board. So a pet dog was butchered for the captain's meals. Cook soon recuperated.

During the following year, Cook gathered data for map-makers as he explored Easter Island and Tonga, New Caledonia, the New Hebrides, and the Marquesas.

On his way back to England he sailed around South Georgia. By doing so he was the first to circumnavigate an Antarctic island.

Cook's second voyage, the most famous of the three, is even more remarkable as he actually traveled not only around the world again, but actually travelled over 96,500 kilometres, or more than three times the circumference of the planet.

Map of New Zealand, in *Atlas of the World*, Rome, 1798.
Sforzesco Castle, Milan.

A Man of the Sandwich Islands in a Mask.
Plate 66 from *A Voyage to the Pacific Ocean*, 1784.
James Cook (1728-1779).
Coloured engraving.
Private collection.

During a year ashore, Cook learned of the latest navigational instruments, and especially of a highly accurate chronometer for use with new nautical tables for establishing longitude. It is remarkable that Cook achieved what he did during his first two voyages before the availability of these greatly improved instruments.

Cook's Third Voyage

Cook was now ready to accept the Admiralty's invitation on behalf of Britain to search yet again for a navigable waterway between the world's two largest oceans, but this time from the Pacific side. There was apparently some notion that the desired passage might be accessed somehow from the west, if not from the east.

The second part of Cook's assignment was to take livestock to the farmers in some of the colonies in the Pacific, gifts from King George III. In his own country King George was known somewhat less than respectfully as 'Farmer George' on account of his interest in agricultural improvements which were contemporarily causing the population of England to rise dramatically.

Probably because of popular movies, many of us know that George III 'was mad'. 'DNA testing of the remains of some of George's descendants has provided evidence for genetic defects being responsible for (the serious disease) porphyria in the British and German royal families.'[29]

Although it is only peripherally relevant to our topic here, some of the same symptoms caused by porphyria are associated with lead poisoning or plumbism.

We will see that this disease was the cause of the deaths of British Arctic explorer John Franklin and his 134 men in 1845.

Meanwhile George's image in the American colonies was anything but positive. In fact, a few days before Cook set sail on his last voyage on 12 July 1776, the Americans formally declared their independence from Britain.

The Age of Discovery was phasing out as it overlapped with the new Age of Revolution. The French would be next with their historic revolution in 1789. The Russian, Chinese and Cuban revolutions would follow.

Four and a half months into this voyage, on 25 December, Cook discovered Christmas Island, the largest atoll in the Pacific. It was not annexed to Great Britain until 1888. (The British would conduct nuclear tests there in 1957 and 1958, and the USA would continue from 1962.)

Cook Landing at Tanna, One of the New Hebrides, c. 1775-1776.
William Hodges (1744-1797).
Oil on canvas.
National Maritime Museum, Greenwich.

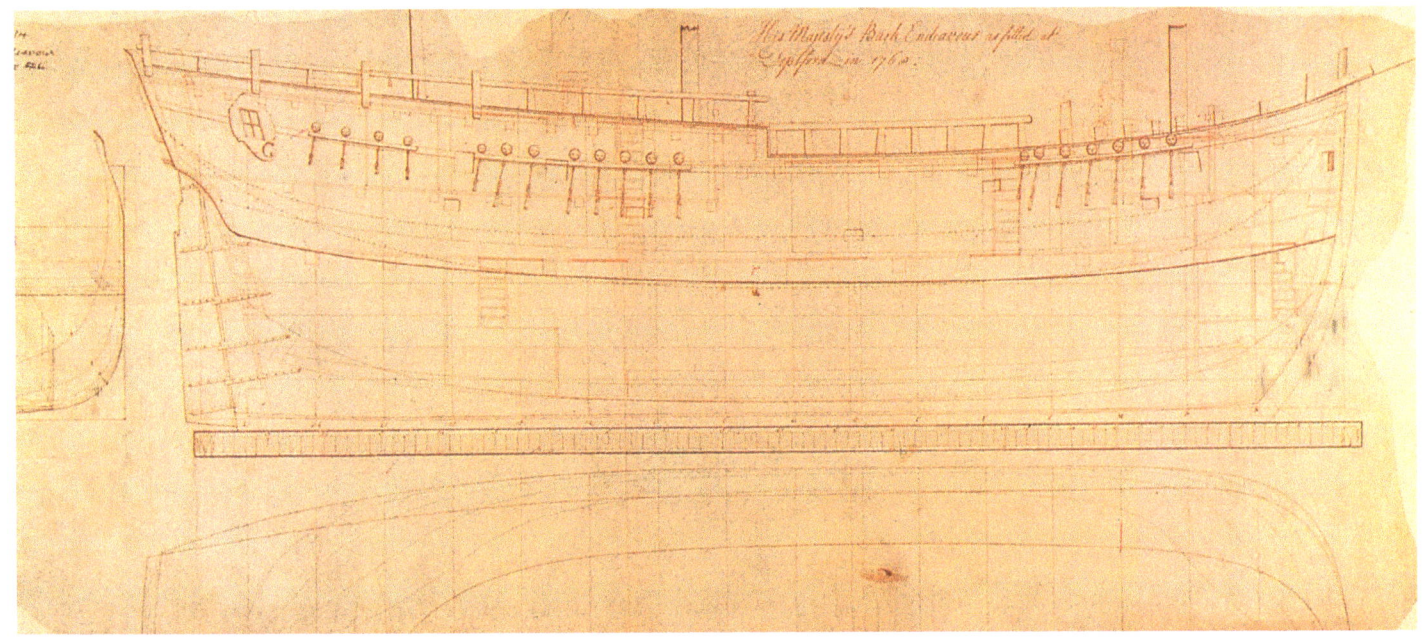

Cook then discovered the islands that he named the Sandwich Islands, after the notorious and very unpopular John Montague, fourth Earl of Sandwich who was the First Lord of the British Admiralty.

The Sandwich Islands would later be renamed the Hawaiian Islands. However, it may be that Cook was not actually the first European to discover the islands.[30]

Having delivered livestock to the island farmers, he moved on to the more important challenge of his assignment: finding a northern passage from the Pacific to the Atlantic. He sailed east to North America, landing at Nootka Sound, near Vancouver.

Continuing up the west American coast, Cook finally passed through the Bering Strait before meeting icepacks that blocked him from further advance. Still, he gathered data missing from the charts of the strait, the first charts made since those by the Danish captain, Vitus Bering, who had been to the area nearly fifty years earlier.

Upon Cook's return to Hawaii, the natives made out that they considered him to be the reincarnation of one of their gods. (It was rather reminiscent of Cortés' being considered a messiah-figure by the Aztecs in around 1520, except Cook had no intention of encouraging or exploiting the natives' simple faith.)

However, the natives then inexplicably stole one of Cook's small boats. Cook's seizure of a tribal chief as a hostage for the boat created a riot among

Plan of the Endeavour, ship of James Cook's expedition in 1768.

Portrait of Captain James Clarke Ross.
Admiral Sir James Clarke Ross (1800-1862).
Pastel and watercolour.
Royal Geographical Society, London.

Map of the Port-des-Français, in L'Atlas du voyage de la Pérouse, 1797.
Private Collection.

Louis XVI Giving Instructions to the Captain La Pérouse, for his Voyage of Exploration Around the World in the Presence of the Marquis de Castries, Ministry of the Navy, 29 June 1785, 1817. Nicolas André Monsiau (1754-1837).
Oil on canvas, 272 x 227 cm.
Château de Versailles, Versailles.

the natives, during which Cook was killed. It was an ironic end for a non-violent man. It was also 'an uncanny re-enactment of the death of Magellan so many years before.'[31]

The expedition sailed north again to the Bering Strait for another try at the fabled northern passage, but it eventually was stopped by ice.

Once again it turned south, this time it followed the Asian profile past Japan, across the Indian Ocean, around the southern tip of Africa (Cape Agulhas) and back to the British Isles, this time sailing up the English Channel to the east coast, unlike the two previous returns.

We have noticed how some explorers during the Age of Discovery were still not yet thirty years old when making their final voyages. Cook, however, was already forty years old when he accepted the tremendous challenge of his three most formidable voyages. Most men of his day were past their physical prime by that age, if not earlier.

Yet in his final ten years alone, 'Cook's achievements might well have occupied the lifetimes of a dozen lesser men.'[32]

JEAN-FRANÇOIS DE LA PEROUSE

During the first decade of American independence, the future forty-ninth state of the United States was visited in 1786 by a French expedition – an expedition approved by Louis XVI and commanded by Jean-François de La Pérouse, appointed captain four years earlier at the age of forty. He reached the west coast of Alaska. Portolani of the coastlines between Monterey and Alaska were developed in an effort to continue the work of Cook as the French made further claims to north-western territories. The French did not establish sovereignty in this region. However, La Pérouse was one of the 'discoverers' of the eastern coast of New Caledonia. He and his two ships were lost in a Pacific storm in 1789.[33]

JOHN AND JAMES ROSS

The British Arctic explorer and rear admiral John Ross, born in Scotland in 1777, set out in search of the North-west Passage in 1818. With him was his nephew, James Clark Ross, who himself also later became a rear admiral and an Arctic explorer (see above). They reached only as far as Baffin Bay, confirming the

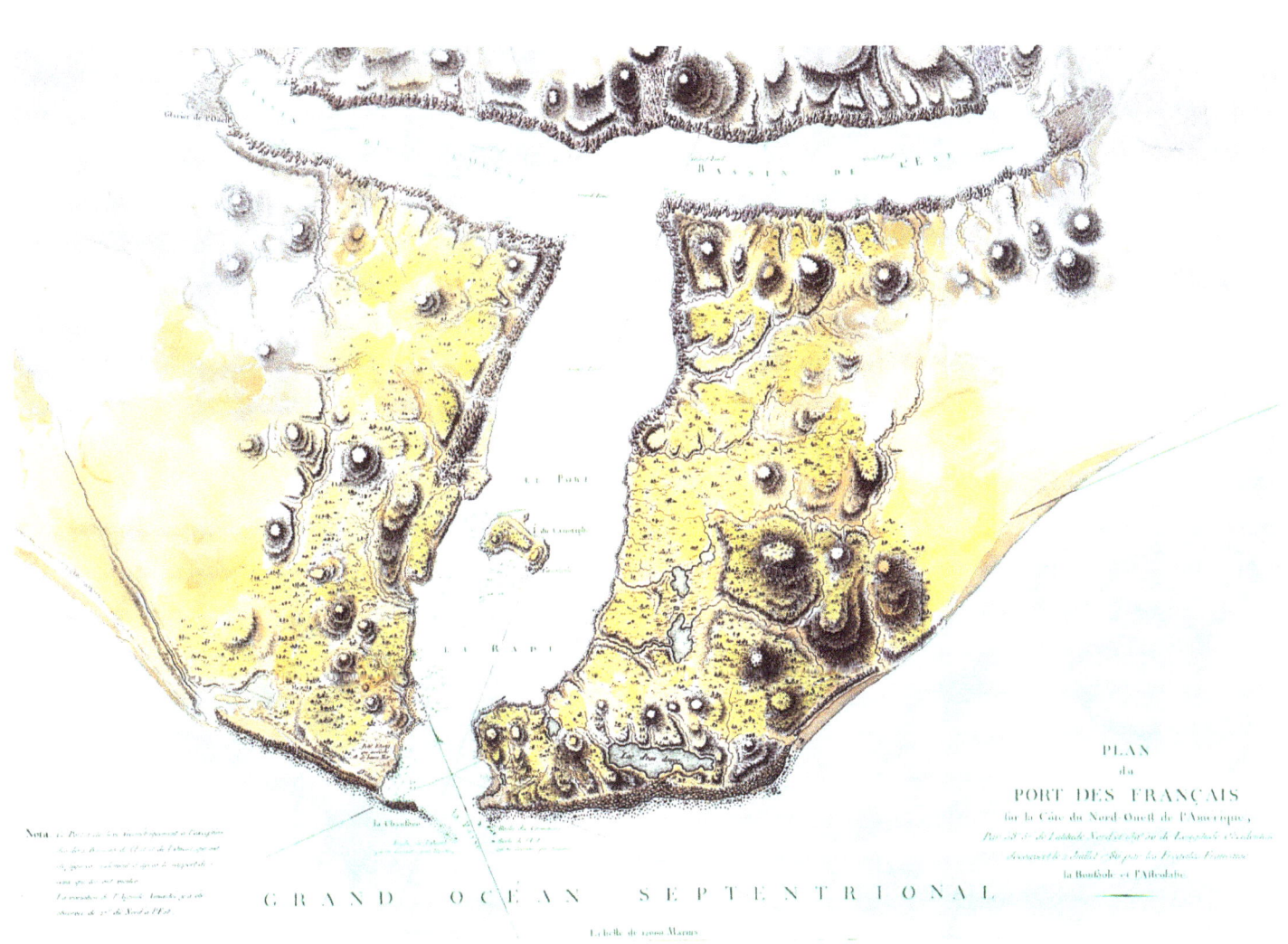

discovery of British explorer William Baffin in 1616. Baffin had been also searching for that elusive northern waterway, but he came to believe it did not exist, a conviction that might have discouraged subsequent expeditions for some time. But neither John nor James Ross was ever put off because of previous failures.

We will see that they each would similarly search for a lost expedition, even though dozens of attempts had failed before.

On a second expedition (1829-1833) with his uncle, James Ross discovered the north magnetic pole on the present Prince of Wales Island. In an age with fewer monumental discoveries, this would surely have received more notice.

Meanwhile, the elder Ross discovered Boothia Peninsula and the Gulf of Boothia, both named after his financial backer, Felix Booth. John Ross also discovered King William Island – named after the British King William IV (third son of George III), whose reign began shortly after the expedition began – and explored the far north, naming Smith Sound, Jones Sound and Lancaster Sound.

Besides sailing with his uncle, James Ross had accompanied William Parry on several voyages, and in his own expeditions to the Antarctic James Ross discovered the sea, island, and shelf ice-sheet, each to be named Ross. He also discovered Victoria Land and a portion of North Graham Land.

After publishing his voyages and research experiences in 1847, just as his uncle had published his own experiences in 1835, he made an unsuccessful visit to the Arctic again in search of the lost British explorer John Franklin and his men. His uncle, in his final trip to the Arctic, failed in the same quest the following year.[34]

JOHN FRANKLIN

More than forty expeditions over the years searched unsuccessfully for the British explorer John Franklin and his 134 men. Eventually, between 1857 and 1859, John Rae and Francis McClintock (who had been with Franklin on an earlier expedition) determined that ships they found frozen in the ice between Victoria Island and King William Island were indeed those of Franklin. Documents in metal tubes left behind by the expedition were buried under rocks and covered over with wooden markers.

They told what had happened to the expedition, including the fact that Franklin had died in 1847. Other men also perished and were buried near the markers. Still others set out to travel south across the frozen surface... but there are no known survivors.

Map of New Holland (Australia) and New Guinea, in *Atlas of the World*, Rome, 1798.
Sforzesco Castle, Milan.

Sir John Franklin, c. 1830.
William Derby (1786-1847).
Watercolour, 222 x 181 cm.
Greenwich Hospital Collection,
National Maritime Museum,
Greenwich.

Like Columbus, who died apparently convinced that he had reached the West Indies, the members of the Franklin expedition surely died thinking they had not reached the North-west Passage. Ironically, they had!

Even in his own day Franklin was a living link to other times. As a teenager he had fought in the famous sea battle at Trafalgar off the coast of Spain in 1805. The British, under the great Horatio Nelson, defeated the French and Spanish fleets, ending Napoleon's control of the seas, and making the much-feared invasion of England by the French impossible.

At Trafalgar, Nelson's comparatively small flagship, *HMS Victory*, was 69 metres long – longer than the typical Engish warship (46 metres) of the seventeenth century, but shorter than even a Roman galley (72 metres). (For details see *Comparisons*, Diagram Group, St Martin's Press, New York, 1980.)

With ingenious naval strategy, the underdog British captured twenty enemy ships without losing one of their own – although Nelson was killed in the famous battle. It would be about 150 years before the mystery of Franklin's expedition would be solved. In 1984, anthropologist Owen Beattie of the University of Alberta would find the Franklin site. Autopsies on three well-preserved frozen bodies revealed that the Franklin men died of lead poisoning.

The expedition was among the first ever to use canned food. Unfortunately, the technology of canning was primitive at the time; the cans were lined with lead that contaminated the food. Scientists would only later learn that poisoning from lead causes anaemia, constipation, colic, paralysis, dementia or death.

There was evidence also of cannibalism, as was revealed in 1987 by Beattie and John Geiger in their book *Frozen in Time: Unlocking the Secrets of the Franklin Expedition*. (The book is written for children but is guaranteed to hold adult interest as well.)

There is also video-program documentation that shows the use of advanced medical technologies to solve the mystery of the Franklin expedition.

JAMES KNIGHT

Also by Beattie and Geiger is *Dead Silence* (1991), a study that describes the tragedy of the Englishman James Knight's voyage to Hudson's Bay in 1719. Then in his seventies, Knight with two ships and forty men was seeking the North-west Passage. Like Franklin's expedition, Knight's was also lost and evidence not found for three centuries. During four seasons of investigation, Beattie and Geiger found

The Friendly Islands, in *Atlas of the World*, Rome, 1798. Sforzesco Castle, Milan.

the ship's remains submerged in the Arctic near Marble Island, known to the Inuit as 'Dead Man's Island', off the north-west coast of Hudson's Bay. No significant forensic conclusion about the fate of Knight or his sailors has been made.[35]

WILLIAM EDWARD PARRY

In 1790, the British naval officer George Vancouver explored the north-west coast of North America, from San Francisco to British Columbia. Both Vancouver Island and Vancouver, British Columbia, are named for him.

The year 1790 was also the birth year of another British naval officer and explorer, William Edward Parry. While a naval lieutenant, Parry proved himself to be a serious yet innovative scientist. After making many careful astronomical observations in the northern latitudes he published *Nautical Astronomy by Night* in 1816. Even though he was only twenty-six, his work earned respect and notice from colleagues.

Participating in the Arctic expedition of explorer John Ross in 1818, Parry had command of a brig. Although that expedition was unsuccessful, the experience contributed over the next twelve months toward his obtaining the chief command of two ships for his own Arctic expedition.

Parry's Second Voyage

Later that same year Parry led a second expedition to pioneer the North-west Passage, but it too failed to make it through, and he returned in 1823. The following year, with the same ships he was again unsuccessful, this time returning with both crews aboard one ship because the other ship had been wrecked.

When in 1827 the British finally shifted their sights from the attained practicality of reaching the Pacific from the East to the as yet elusive glory of reaching the North Pole, Parry was commissioned to attempt a voyage to that northern extremity.

While he is forever associated with endeavouring to attain that goal, ironically the most northern point Parry ever reached was in fact latitude 82° 45' North.

Parry died in 1855. The human drive to explore and discover for 'God, glory or greed' lived on, for that year Scottish missionary, physician and explorer David Livingston discovered Victoria Falls and the Zambezi River. In 1856 he was at least the first non-African, if not the first man, to cross the continent from its west coast to the Indian Ocean.

Nordenskiöld's Ships, The Vega and Lena Saluting the Cape Chelyuskin, 19 August 1878. Coloured Engraving.

Polar Dress and Eskimo's Eyewear.

Critical Position of H.M.S. Investigator on the North-Coast of Baring Island, 20 August 1851, in *A Series of Eight Sketches in Colour of the Voyage of H.M.S. Investigator*, London, 1854. Samuel Gurney Cresswell. Royal Geographical Society, London.

The Sea, 1864.
Ivan Aivazovsky (1817-1900).
Oil on canvas, 129 x 179 cm.
Aivazovsky Museum, Feodosia.

Also that year, the United States naval officer Matthew Fontaine Maury, 'the pathfinder of the seas,' published in two volumes with four maps the first text description of deep-sea oceanography, *The Physical Geography of the Sea*, a monumental achievement. Matthew Maury's third son, Mytton Maury, later published a revised edition of his father's most famous work. Existing papers show that Mytton was planning to publish yet another revision, making many corrections to errors in the previous editions. However, his unfinished work at the moment remains unpublished.[36]

Robert Peary

A year after the publication of Maury's seminal work on oceans, Pennsylvanian Robert Peary was born. When he was thirty years old Peary became intensely interested in the Arctic. In 1886, during a decade when many adventurous people were becoming more interested in inventions of electrical and mechanical things than in geographical exploration, Peary visited the interior of Greenland. Five years later he set out on one of his several scientific expeditions to the northerly part of that enormous island. Myths and superstitions about the northlands may be seen illustrated in portolani, but Peary proved that safe and economical expeditions could be made.

By 1889, Peary was prepared to search for the North Pole, but, like his near-namesake Parry before him, on his early attempts he did not reach the ultimate point. At first he reached 84° 17' North. Then, about five years later, he reached 87° 6' North, less than 282 kilometres from his goal.

Finally and successfully, with a servant and four Eskimos, he reached the North Pole in 1909. That same year US naturalist Roy Chapman Andrews led a scientific expedition to Alaska. Interest in the northern and southern extremes was dramatically pushing geographical exploration to its ultimate limits on the surface of the Earth.

Returning to the USA from the North Pole, Peary received the disquieting news that the surgeon who had accompanied him on his 1891 expedition (F. A. Cook) had claimed that he had reached the North Pole in 1908. It took a couple years, but in 1911 Congress recognised Robert Peary's claim. Only later did scientific investigations prove his achievement.

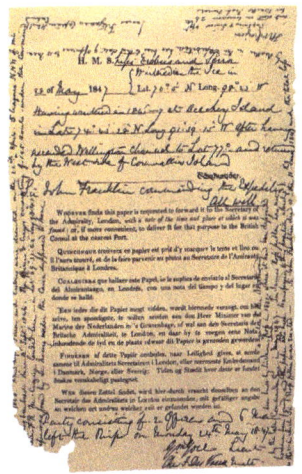

The American Explorer Frederick Cook Planting the United-States Flag in North Pole, in La Domenica del Corriere, 12 September 1909. Achille Beltrame.

ROALD AMUNDSEN

That same year, Norwegian Roald Amundsen was also the first man to reach the South Pole. However, his earlier achievement in 1906 was the one Europe had been working towards for centuries.

Taking three years, from 1903 to 1906, he finally broke through the many ice barriers that separated the Atlantic from the Pacific. The North-west Passage was at last no longer just a theory. The South Pole has been the site of some highly significant scientific discoveries in recent years (1999-2000) by biologist Ed Carpenter and his team, who have succeeded in discovering thousands of minute organisms that appear to be surviving perfectly happily in a climate previously thought to be incapable of sustaining life.

Doug Capone of the University of Southern California points out that the physical environment at the South Pole comprises many conditions similar to those that once pertained on the planet Mars. To study Antarctica is one way to find out whether life is or was possible on Mars.

Such research might also lead to methodological improvements in the cryogenic storage of live human organs for future transplants.

Facsimile of the letter left by the Franklin expedition that notes where they abandoned the ships and the death of Franklin, in *The Voyage of the 'Fox' in the Arctic Seas: A Narrative of the Discovery of the Fate of Sir John Franklin and His Companions*, 1859.
The Mariners' Museum, Newport News.

Sled Dogs Sitting on the Snow at the South Pole,
14 December 1911, 1911.
Roald Amundsen.
Photograph in black and white, sepia toned,
12.6 x 8.2 cm.
National Library of Australia, Canberra.

Explorers' Lifelines

Sailing Towards the Modern World: 1700 – 1900

Den	Vitus Bering	[1681–1741]
Spa	Gaspar de Portola	[c.1723–c.1784]
Eng	James Cook	[1728–1779]
Fra	Louis Antoine de Bougainville	[1729–1811]
Fra	Jean-François de La Pérouse	[1741–1788]
Sco	Alexander Mackenzie	[c.1755–1820]
Us	Robert Gray	[1755–1806]
Eng	George Vancouver	[c.1757–1798]
Eng-Can	David Thompson	[c.1770–1857]
Us	William Clark	[1770–1838]
Us	Meriwether Lewis	[1774–1809]
Eng	John Ross	[1777–1856]
Us	Oliver Hazard Perry	[1785–1819]
Eng	James Weddell	[c.1787–1834]
Eng	William E. Parry	[1790–1855]
Rus	Ferdinand Wrangel	[1796–1870]
Us	Charles Wilkes	[1798–1877]
Us	Nathaniel Palmer	[1799–1877]
Eng	Richard Burton	[1821–1890]
Eng	Samuel White Baker	[1821–1893]
Us	Robert Peary	[1856–1920]
Us	Matthew Henson	[1866–1955]
Eng	Robert F. Scott	[1868–1912]
Nor	Roald Amundsen	[1872–1928]
Us	Donald Macmillan	[1874–1970]
Us	Robert Bartlett	[1875–1946]
Us	Vilhjalmur Stefansson	[1879–1962]
Us	Roy Andrews	[1884–1960]
Aus	George Hubert Wilkins	[c.1888–1958]
Us	Richard Byrd	[1888–1957]
Fra	Jacques-Yves Cousteau	[1910–1997]
Nor	Thor Heyerdahl	[1914–]

CONCLUSION

US Explorers

Once the dust settled after the American Revolutionary War (1775–1783), the next generation of Americans was eager to explore its new land and other horizons. It was as if it had to rush to catch up with centuries of discoveries and achievements already enjoyed by the rest of the world.

Looking through the list of the forty-eight major United States explorers who lived during the eighteenth and nineteenth centuries, we see that more than half (actually twenty-seven) of them would spend their energies on exploring the land that was, or would eventually be, their own country.

At the end of that period, 10 percent (five) of them would research into and advance air exploration. And much further into the last century of the millennium, another quarter of those US explorers would be pioneers in the exploration of space.

Only 10 percent (six) United States explorers would continue researching into the mysteries of the oceans, continuing a process well established by older nations.

American exploration began by stretching westward on land, following the Louisiana Purchase (1803). The boundaries were pushed still further west toward the Pacific by Lewis and Clarke (1804–1806). The adventurous men and women of the new nation were then already reaching outward by sea.

From 1787 to 1790 Robert Gray captained the first US ship to circumnavigate the globe. In 1792 came the discovery of the Columbia River in Oregon.

Two generations later Charles Wilkes led an around-the-world expedition (1838–1842), went down into the Antarctic and discovered Wilkes Land. As the commander of a Union warship during the US Civil War, he stopped the British mail steamer Trent and arrested two passengers who were Confederate commissioners, taking them on to Boston where they were imprisoned.

Because the halting of the ship and the arrest of the men was technically piracy, the event ('the Trent Affair') became the subject of a very hasty smoothing-over operation by the US and British governments of the time.

The American heroes of the polar regions were men and women born only a few years after the American Revolution: Palmer and Wilkes. They would advance humankind's knowledge of the frozen continents during the first half of the nineteenth century.

After them, six future American explorers of the Arctic were born late in the century. One, Robert Edwin Peary, would begin the next century by opening the frozen door even further, inspiring a dozen US explorers to continue his work well into the 1900s.

Taking up the intense interest of nineteenth-century Europeans in exploring the polar extremes, the USA soon became a major competitor, producing some of the 20th century's greatest Arctic explorers since Palmer, Peary and Wilkes. These included Richard Evelyn Byrd, Lincoln Ellsworth, Matthew Henson, Donald Baxter McMillan, and Vilhjalmur Stefansson. Their lifelines and dates of major events are charted here.

Early interest in polar exploration was enthusiastically followed by popular culture as newspaper and magazine reports kept detailing the expeditions. By 1907, G. Firth Scott was already writing about expeditions to both Poles in *The Romance of Polar Exploration*.[37]

Us Arctic Explorers

	Born	Major events	Died
Wilkes	1796	1838, 1842, 1861	1877
Palmer	1799	1820, 1822	1877
Peary	1856	1886, 1893–94, 1909	1920
Henson	1866	1909	1955
McMillan	1874	1909, 1913, 1937	1970
Stefansson	1879	1908, 1918	1962
Ellsworth	1880	1926, 1935	1951
Byrd	1888	1926, 1928, 1956	1957

Snow, Storm. Steam-Boat off a Harbour's Mouth, 1842.
Joseph Mallord William Turner (1775-1851).
Oil on canvas, 91.4 x 121.9 cm.
Tate Gallery, London.

Seascape, Moonlight, 1878.
Ivan Aivazovsky (1817-1900).
Oil on canvas, 213.5 x 148 cm.
The Russian Museum, St Petersburg.

Chronology Of US Explorations

1820	Palmer the first European to see Antarctica
1822	Palmer helps discover South Orkney Island
1838	Wilkes discovers Wilkes Land
1886	Peary explores Greenland ice-sheet
1893	Peary explores Greenland ice-sheet again
1893	Josephine Peary publishes her account
1905	Bartlett commands Peary's ship
1908	McMillan travels with Peary on Arctic expedition
1908	Stefansson explores Canadian Arctic
1909	Henson places US flag near North Pole
1909	Peary's first expedition nears North Pole
1913	Stefansson adapts to Eskimo life style; demythologises the Far North
1913	McMillan leads several Arctic expeditions
1914	Bartlett reaches Siberia
1926	Ellsworth leads first transArctic air crossings
1926	Ellsworth lead first crossing of the polar basin
1926–32	Bartlett heads expeditions of Greenland, Baffin Island, Labrador
1926	Byrd makes first flight over North Pole
1928	Byrd pioneers aerial mapping of Arctic
1931	Ellsworth claims 300,000 square miles of Antarctica for USA
1935	Ellsworth leads first transantarctic air crossings
1956	Byrd ends his Arctic expeditions

In 1926, Norwegian Roald Amundsen was also the first to cross the Arctic by air. The next year Charles Lindbergh was the first to make a solo nonstop transatlantic flight, from New York to Paris.

The world was truly becoming smaller, and peoples were discovering each other at an increasingly rapid pace.

The following year American ethnologist Vilhjalmur Stefansson adapted to the Eskimo lifestyle, destroying many myths about the Arctic archipelago's being utterly inhospitable. Probably nobody demonstrated that fact more than Peary's wife, Josephine.

Women On Board

After her husband's death, the wife of Alvaro de Mendaña de Neyra (1541–1696) continued to lead his second expedition into the Philippines. She was one of the few women ever to be directly involved in the exploration of the seas – other than the rare female pirate (if we may include piracy along with bona fide exploration).

The most notorious female pirates were Mary Read and Anne Bonny, the latter described by a contemporary as 'profligate, cursing and swearing much, and very ready and willing to do anything on board' – see David Cordingly, *Under the Black Flag. op. cit.*

However, surely no woman was more dramatically involved in exploration than Josephine Diebitsch Peary, who accompanied her husband on several of the historic expeditions.

In her book *Arctic Journal: My Year Among Ice Fields and Eskimos*,[38] published in 1893, Mrs Peary documented her experiences, which included giving birth in the Arctic to their daughter – an event that might be the ultimate symbol of the explorer's conquest of the vast Earth and its unending challenges.

From heroic action on spectacular expeditions around the globe, to the quiet birth of a baby in the vast Arctic, the explorers of the past thousand years gradually completed the map of the planet and moved us onward into the age of space exploration – and now cyberspace exploration.

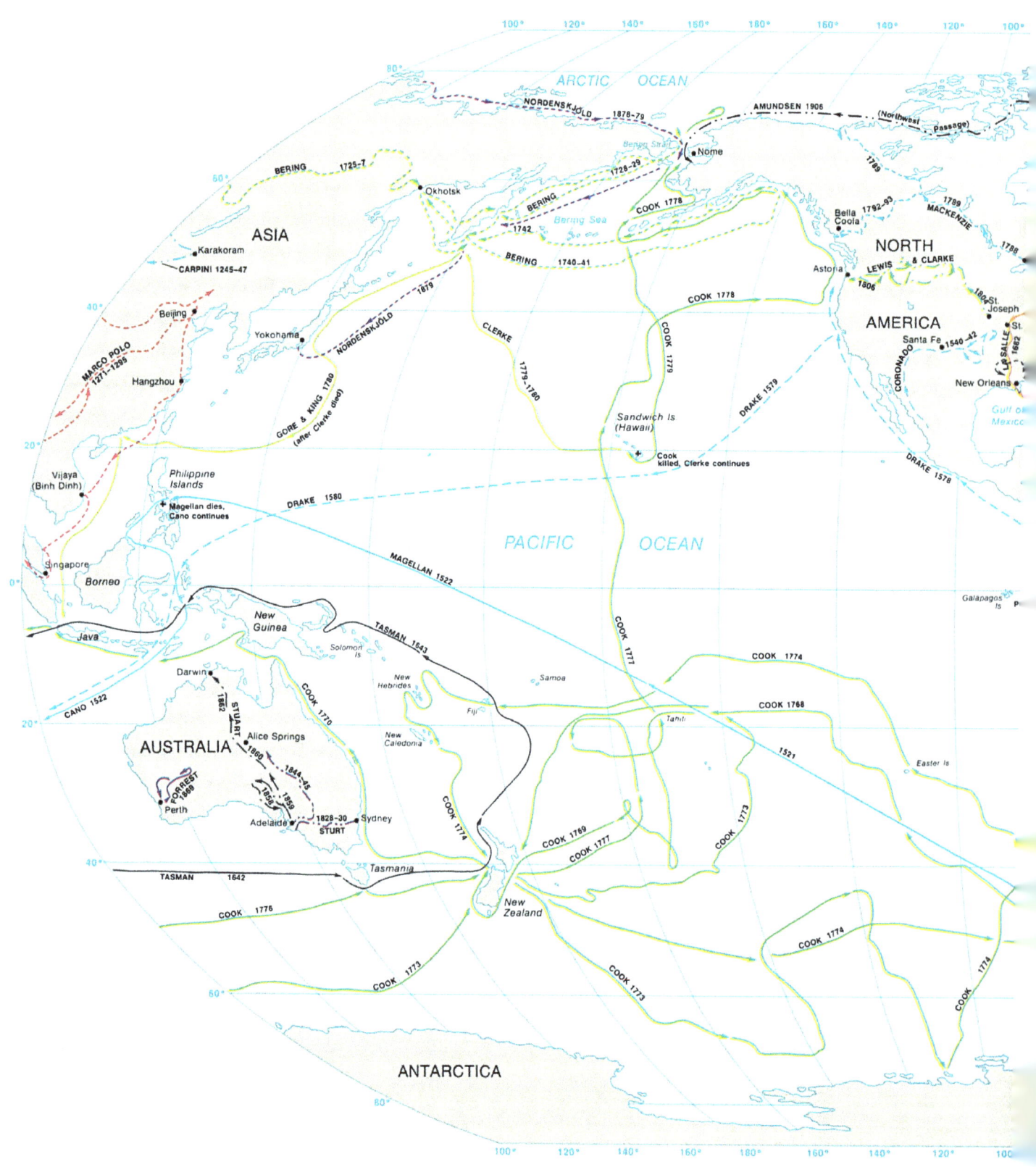

Map of the Major Maritime Explorations.

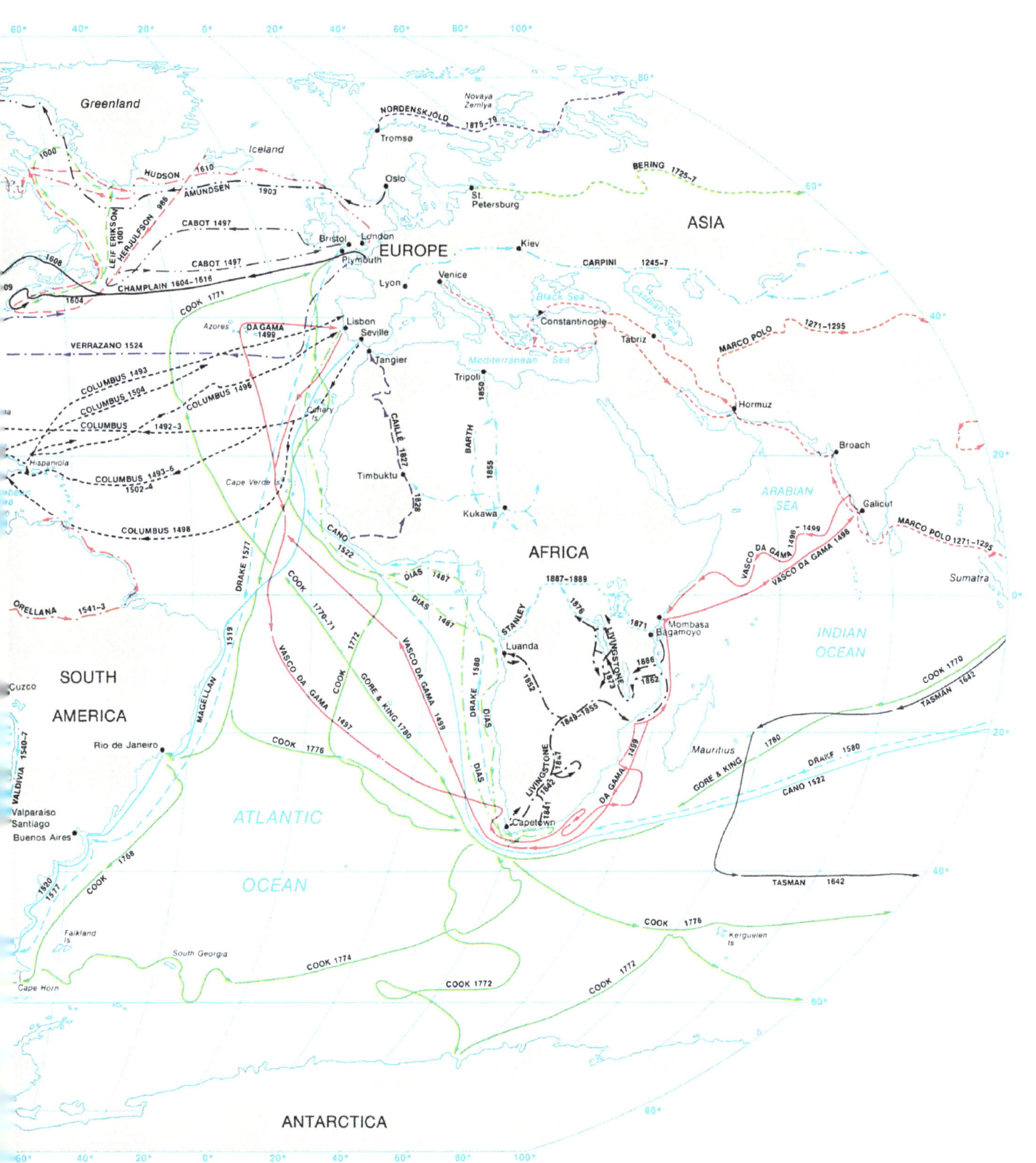

NOTES

1. Herman Melville, *Moby Dick*, Random House, New York, 1930; chapter CLIV.

2. Alexander Pushkin, *Boris Godunov*, 1825; translation by Alfred Hayes.

3. Alan G. Hodgkiss, *Discovering Antique Maps*, Shire, Buckinghamshire (UK), 1971; page 28.

4. See 'The Voyages to Vinland,' translated by A. M. Reeves, *American Historical Documents 1000–1904*, *The Harvard Classics*, Grolier, Danbury CT, 1980. (The term doegr is used in the translation apparently for a period of time that is distinct from a day. DW)

5. *Ibid.*

6. See Dom Columba Cary-Elwes, *China and the Cross: A Survey of Missionary History*, Kennedy, New York, 1956. For a study of 17th-century Roman Catholic missionary work in China, see Bernard H. Willeke, *Imperial Government and Catholic Missions in China*, Franciscan Institute, New York, 1948.

7. W. Arens, *The Man-Eating Myth: Authropology and Anthropophagy*, New York, 1969. Quoted in Richard Zacks, *An Underground Education*, Doubleday, New York, 1997; page 352.

8. Ernle Bradford, *A Wind From the North: The Life of Henry the Navigator*, Harcourt, Brace, New York, 1960. Richard H. Major, *The Discoveries of Prince Henry the Navigator, and Their Results, Being the Narrative of the Discovery by Sea, Within One Century, of More Than Half the World*, Sampson Low, Marston, Searle & Rivington, London (UK), 1877.

9. Zacks, *op.cit.*; page 347.

10. All comments on portolani in this book are based on informal translation from the Italian of passages in the authoritative resource *I Portolani: Carte nautiche dal XIII al XVII secolo*, by Monique de la Ronciceré, Bramante Arte, 1992. Any incorrect or incomplete statements made here must be regarded as my responsibility mine and not to be found in that resource. DW

11. Zacks, *op.cit.*; page 359.

12. 'Teaching Myths and History', *The New York Times*, editorial, February 17, 1998.

13. 'Amerigo Vespucci's Account of His First Voyage,' translated by M. K. for Quaritch's Editions, London, 1885. Slightly edited here. (This and the other early documents quoted in this chapter are excerpted in the *Harvard Classics* series cited above. DW.)

14. Amerigo Vespucci, *Letters from a New World: Amerigo Vespucci's Discovery of America*, edited by Luciano Formisano, New York, 1992. Quoted at length in Zacks, *op.cit.*; pages 350–352.

15. 'John Cabot's Discovery of North America', from the Hakluyt Society's edition of *Columbus' Journal*.

16. The ship passenger and crew lists from John Fiske's *The Discovering of America*, 1892, are posted at www.enoch.com/genealogy/passenger/htm.

17. Lloyd A. Brown, *The Story of Maps*, Dover, New York, 1979; page 156.

18. 'The Letter of Columbus to Luis de Sant Angel Announcing His Discovery', translated as in American *History Leaflets*, edited by Professors Hart and Channing.

19. Peter Whitfield, *New Found Lands: Maps in the History of Exploration*, Routledge, New York, 1998; page 60. An authoritative and indispensable reference.

20. Zachs, *op.cit.*; page 346.

21. Angus Konstam, *Historical Atlas of Exploration 1492–1600*, Checkmark Books, New York, 2000.

22. Zacks, *op.cit.*; page 347.

23. Whitfield, *op.cit.*; page 68.

24 Warwick Bray, 'Quetzalcóatl', *Academic American Encyclopedia*, Vol. 16, page 24.

25 In his excellent work *Under the Black Flag: The Romance and the Reality of Life Among the Pirates* (New York: Random House, New York, 1999), Dr David Cordingly notes that the word buccaneer was originally applied to hunters of wild oxen and pigs. His work includes full descriptions of all the relevant terms.

26 Edgar Maclay, *The History of American Privateers*, New York, 1899. As quoted in Zacks, *op.cit.*; page 360.

27 Whitfield, *op.cit.*; page 141.

28 G. E. R. Deacon (ed.) *Seas, Maps and Men: An Atlas-History of Man's Exploration of the Oceans*, Doubleday, New York, 1962. We follow here this textbook's chronology of the voyages, with additional reference to subsequent works, including J. Beaglehole's *The Life of Captain James Cook* (1974). Beaglehole also edited the journals of Cook in four volumes, 1955–67.

29 Martin Warren and David Hunt, 'Why Did George III Go Mad?' *Science Spectra*, Number 18, 1999. See also I. Macalpine and R. Hunter, *George III and the Mad Business*, Penguin, London, 1969.

30 Our more familiar use of the word sandwich comes from that Earl's popularising the ancient Roman practice of placing food between slices of bread. The Earl was fond of the practice because it allowed him to continue to eat even while at the gaming table. Cf. Charles Earle Funk, *Thereby Hangs a Tale: Stories of Curious Word Origins*, Colophon, New York, 1950; pages 248–249.

31 Whitfield, *op.cit.*; page 124.

32 John Ross, *Narrative of a Second Voyage in Search of a North-West Passage, and of a Residence in the Arctic Regions During the Years 1829–1833, Including the Reports of Commander, Now Captain, James Clark Ross ...*, A. W. Webster, London, 1835. Six maps, 51 plates, glossary of English, Danish and Eskimo terms. Cf. *Relation du second voyage fait à la recherche d'un passage au Nord Ouest par Sir John Ross...*, Wouters et Cie, Brussels, 1844.

33 Cf. Musée La Pérouse (Albi, France) and the La Pérouse society.

34 Owen Beattie and John Geiger, *Frozen in Time: The Fate of the Franklin Expedition*, Bloomsbury Publishing, London, 1987. See also episode number 19 of the television series *USHUAIA: The Ultimate Adventure*, which includes footage from a documentary about the Franklin location, three graves, the unearthing of a sailor, an autopsy, and other evidence of the lead poisoning.

35 Owen Beattie and John Gieger, *Dead Silence: The Greatest Mystery in Arctic Discovery*, Viking, Toronto, 1991. See also S. C. Gilfillin, 'Lead Poisoning and the Fall of Rome', *Journal of Occupational Medicine*, 7, 53–70 (1965).

36 John W. Wayland, *The Pathfinder of the Seas: The Life of Matthew Fontaine Maury*, Garrett, Richmond VA, 1930.

37 G. Firth Scott, *The Romance of Polar Exploration*, Lon Society, 1907.

38 Josephine Peary, *Arctic Journal: My Year Among Ice Fields and Eskimos*, New York, 1893 (contemporary); an 1897 edition is also available via www.bibliofind.com.

Main resources

This book is intended as a general introduction and as such does not include detailed information on the specific artists responsible for portolani. These and other such related data are given in the authoritative resources of Roger Hervé's original presentation in *Revue d'histoire économique et sociale* (XLV, 197) as illustrated under the heading 'Filiazione delle Scuole idrogafiche' in I Portolani: *Carte nautiche dal XIII al XVII secolo* by Monique de la Ronciéré, Bramante Arte, 1992. The general descriptions of portolani schools and their influences that are given throughout this book are based almost exclusively on those resources. DW

Maritime Museums

Curators from 26 of the maritime museums of the world describe their collections in *Great Maritime Museums of the World*, edited by Peter Neill and Barbara Krohn, Balsam Press, with Harry N. Abrams, 1991.

INDEX

Nations and Eras of Representative Maps in This Book

Dates		Italy, Portugal, Spain	Netherlands	France	Great Britain
1500	Maps	22-25 29-34 37-46 52-54	47		
1600	Maps	85-86	75-87	69	99-100

Map numbers represent an estimated chronological order as well as their location in this book.

Geographical areas

A coastline of each of the following geographical areas is identified on one or more of the antique maps in this work. The numbers refer to maps, not pages. The current names for these areas are used here, as in *The Great Geographical Atlas* of Rand McNally (1982).

Years	1290-1400	1400-1450	1450-1500	1500-1550	1550-1600	1600-1650	1650-1700
Maps	1-10	11-16	17-21	22-44	45-65	66-86	87-100
World				22 26 37 41 42	47 51 55 58 63	81 84	
Northern Europe		12	19 21	22 25 26 27 37 40 41 42 43	47 46 51 55 58 63	70 73 79 80 81 84	91

Years	1290–1400	1400–1450	1450–1500	1500–1550	1550–1600	1600–1650	1650–1700
British Isles	6 8	12		22 25 26 37 41 42 43	47 46 51 52 55 58 63	70 73 78 79 81 83 84	92
France, Belgium, Netherlands	6 10	12		22 26 37 41 42 44	47 51 52 55 58 64	70 73 78 79 81 83 84	
Spain, Portugal	5 8	12	18 19	22 26 37 41 42 43 44	46 51 52 53 55 58 63	70 81 83 84	88
Mediterranean Sea	1 3 4 7 8 9	11 12 15 16	17 18 19	22 23 24 26 37 41 42	47 51 55 56 58 63	66 68 70 79 74 81 84	89
Southern Europe	2	12 13 14		22 24 26 37 41 42	47 51 55 58 63	68 70 81 84	
South-west Asia				22 26 31 37 41 42	47 51 55 58 63 64	72 76 81 84	95 99
South-central Asia				22 26 37 41 42	47 51 55 58 63	81 84	85 87

Years	1290–1400	1400–1450	1450–1500	1500–1550	1550–1600	1600–1650	1650–1700
South-east Asia			22	47 26 32 35 36 37 39 41 42	81 51 54 55 58 59 63 65	96 84	97 98 100
China, Japan			20	22 26 37 41 42	47 51 55 58 63	75 77 81 84 86	
Northern Africa	8			22 27 28 29 34 37	51 26 57 58 63	56 55 81 84	89 70
Western Africa			20	22 25 26 37 38 41 42	46 47 51 55 58 63	71 81 84	88
Southern Africa				22 26 30 37 41 42	47 51 55 58 63	81 84	90 94
Alaska				22 26 37 41 42	47 51 55 58 63	81 83 84 86	
Greenland, Iceland				22 26 37 41 42	47 51 55 58 62 70	79 81 84	

Years	1290–1400	1400–1450	1450–1500	1500–1550	1550–1600	1600–1650	1650–1700
Canada				22 26 37 41 42	47 49 51 55 58 59 63	69 79 81 84	93
Eastern United States				22 25 26 28 37 41 42	46 47 48 49 50 51 55 58 59 63	67 71 81 84	
Western United States				22 25 26 28 37	47 51 55 57 63 41 42	75 81 84	
Central America				22 26 34 37 41 42	45 47 48 51 55 58 62 63	81 84	
South America			22 26 33 37 38 41 42	46 47 51 55 58 60 61 63	67 71 73 75 81 82 84		
Australia				47 55 63	81 84		

See the world maps for other coastal areas, including Antarctic Region and Arctic Region. Those, along with non-coastal areas, are not the main interest of the portolani presented here.

Schools

Century	13th–14th	15th	16th	17th
Genovese	1, 2, 3 4, 5, 6	21	23, 24, 26 41, 56	
Catalan	7, 8, 9	12, 16, 17	62, 64, 65	68
Venetian	10	11, 15 18, 19		76
Spanish			22, 46	
Portuguese			25, 27 29–34 37, 38, 45 52–55, 59 63	73, 81–82 85, 86 94
Istanbul			28, 35, 36	
Normandy			39, 40 47–51	67, 71, 78 80, 84 58, 60, 61
British			42–44	
Greek			57	66
Dutch				70, 75, 79 87, 88, 96
Japanese				72, 77
Marseille				74, 83, 89
Other				90, 93, 95 98, 99, 100
Basque				91, 97
French				92

GLOSSARY

Anthropophagy see cannibalism

Archipelago A group of islands, especially one that forms a geographical unit or recognisable chain, and especially one that is localised within a specific sea or oceanic area.

Astrolabe (from the Greek *aster* 'star' and *labein* 'to take') An astronomical instrument used probably from ancient Greek times to measure the height above the horizon of celestial bodies, and especially at sea to measure the altitude of the sun or a particular star in order to estimate one's approximate latitude. It classically consists of a brass ring fitted with an alidade or sighting rule in the form of a diameter pivoted at the center of the ring. Suspended from a shackle at the top of the ring, the *alidade* was optically aligned with the sun or the star, and the angle was read off against calibrations or gradations on the outer brass ring.

Bearings, compass bearings Coordinates defining either a direction or a precise position. A direction is defined for most people by reference to one or a combination of the four main compass points (from north through east through south through west and back through north), although for navigation it is expressed generally as a number of degrees (and minutes) east of true north. A position is defined by reference to lines of latitude and longitude, and expressed as a number of degrees (and minutes) north or south of the equator followed by the number of degrees (and minutes) west or east of the prime meridian (*see* longitude). *See also* orientation.

Bilge(s) The lowest part inside a vessel's hull – where water in the hull may collect and slop around.

Cannibalism The eating of human flesh, generally roasted or boiled. Very few cultures have engaged in the practice on a regular basis. Those that did usually ate prisoners of war on the principle that the devourers would ingest some of the physical, mental or even spiritual qualities of the devoured. A technical term for cannibalism is *anthropophagy* (from Greek word-elements for 'man-eating').

Caravel A small three-masted vessel developed during the fourteenth century. This adaptable ship might be rigged with a combination of triangular (lateen) and square sails. The *Niña* was a caravel that was rigged like this for extra speed.

Cartographer A person who makes accurate maps and charts. Cartography is the science and practice of projecting by various methods an area of the Earth's surface on a flat plane, such as a sheet of parchment or paper.

Chronometer An extremely accurate clock, especially a mechanical device for keeping time independent of a ship's motion. By knowing exactly when it was noon at Greenwich on the prime meridian (0 degrees longitude – see longitude) and comparing the local time in hours before or after noon, it was possible to judge fairly accurately the distance west or east the location was of the prime meridian – because one hour in time (one twenty-fourth of a day) corresponds to 15 degrees of longitude (one twenty-fourth of the great circle that is a meridian).

Compass In basic form, an instrument in which a magnetised metal needle is allowed to align itself with the locally prevailing magnetic fields of the Earth. This, in most regions, causes one end of the needle to point roughly north. From early times, European mariners have used this instrument to navigate their ships. The Chinese are said to have invented the first compass over 2,000 years ago.

Far East Japan and China and countries in the east of the Asian continent – the far east for Europeans. For western North Americans, of course, the Far East is closer and to the west than some of Europe is to the east.

Lateen sail A triangular sail suspended from a lengthy yard (horizontal spar or boom) on a relatively short mast.

Latitude Of a great circle running 'horizontally' east to west around the surface of the Earth. Lines of latitude determine location north or south on the globe. The longest line of latitude is the equator.

Longitude Of a great circle running 'vertically' north to south around the surface of the Earth, through the Poles. Lines of longitude, or 'meridians', determine location east or west of the prime meridian: the prime meridian is 0 degrees, and is established as passing directly through Greenwich, London, England. See also chronometer.

Mainmast On ships with two or more masts, the mast second from the bow.

Mast A vertical shaft, usually made of wood or metal, that supports the sails. On larger sailing ships, masts are always constructed in two or even three sections (lower masts and topmasts).

Masthead The top of a lower mast, to which a topmast is attached.

Meridian, prime meridian see longitude

Orientation On a map, the direction represented by a vertical line to the top of the map. On most maps today the orientation is to true north. On nautical charts, however, and on portolani, the orientation may for one reason or another be to quite a different direction, in which case a floral symbolisation of a compass (a 'rose') may indicate which direction on the map is actually north, or which direction is represented by a vertical line to the top.

Portolano An old nautical chart or map on which at least some of the information is tentative or downright inaccurate because it is as yet not properly known; portolani may also include illustrations, comments, dedications and other textual matter not normally found on ordinary maps today. The word is Italian.

Quadrant A simple instrument for determining the angular height above the horizon of heavenly bodies such as the sun or a particular star. It comprises a metal frame in the form of a quarter of a circle (hence 'quadrant') with a small weight suspended on a string from its apex. With the straight edge of the frame optically aligned with the sun or the star, the weighted line falls across a calibrated scale marked in degrees from 0 to 90 on the curved edge, indicating the angle of elevation.

Rig, rigging see sail

Roadstead A sheltered anchorage, often a bay or creek that provides calmer water out of prevailing winds and currents.

Rose, compass rose see orientation

Rhumb-line A line across the surface of a globe that intersects all meridians (lines of longitude) at the same angle. Technically, a line of latitude is a special sort of rhumb-line, but the word more usually describes a direct course across an ocean plotted between two landmarks or siting-points.

Sail A large piece of cloth hung from a vessel's mast and designed to catch the wind and use its force to propel the vessel. The many sizes and shapes of sail, the specific sites at which they are positioned on a vessel, and the means by which they are hoisted up or lowered as necessary, all have their own technical terms, but may be generally said to represent the vessel's rig or rigging.

Sandglass A mechanical device for measuring the passage of time as sand (or crushed marble or eggshells) runs gradually from an upper glass chamber to a lower through a constricted neck, taking a predetermined duration of time to do so. Once the sand is all in the lower chamber, the whole de-vice is turned over and the sand starts to flow again. Before chronometers, sandglasses were usually supplied to a ship in four sizes: half-minute, half-hour, one hour and four hours. This is how 'watches' in the navy were originally four hours long, and a bell tolled every half-hour so that the end of one watch and the beginning of the next was eight bells.

Scurvy A disease caused by a lack of vitamin C in the food eaten. Symptoms include swollen and bleeding gums, nausea, weakness, loss of hair and teeth, and gray areas in the skin. Untreated, it may be fatal. In some former centuries more sailors died of this than from any other cause. The limes and lime-juice prescribed by the (British) Royal Navy for its mariners during the 18th century to successfully avoid this disease caused British sailors to become known as 'limeys' by American sailors.

Spice Islands A 16th- to 19th-century European term for the islands that now collectively make up Indonesia.

Square-rigged Using square or rectangular sails on two or more masts.

Terra 'Land' in Latin – the international language of cartographers and scholars in medieval and Renaissance times. Thus *Terra Australis* 'Land of the South', *Terra Incognita* 'Land that is Unknown', *Terra Nigrorum* 'Land of Black People', *Terra Nova* 'Land that is New(-found)', and so on.

Watch see sandglass

FURTHER REFERENCE

Books

Ageton, Arthur, *Manual of Celestial Navigation*. Second revised edition. New York: D. Van Nostrand, 1961.

Albion, Robert Greenhalgh and Pope, Jennie Barnes, *Sea Lanes In Wartime: The American Experience 1775–1945*. Second edition, enlarged. Hamden: Archon, 1968.

Allen, Gay Wilson, *Melville And His World*. New York: Viking, 1971.

Andrews, J. R. H., *The Southern Ark: Zoological Discovery in New Zealand 1769–1900*. Honolulu: University of Hawaii, Honolulu, 1986.

Armstrong, Warren, *Mutiny Afloat: A Dramatised Record of Some Famous Sea Mutinies*. London: Frederick Muller, 1956

Atkinson, Ian, *The Viking Ships*. Cambridge: Cambridge University Press, 1980.

Authwaite, Leonard, *Unrolling the Map*. New York: Reynal & Hitchcock, 1935.

Ball, Ian M. Pitcairn, *Children of Mutiny*. Boston: Little, Brown, 1973 (A study of an extraordinary society, with a new look at the Bounty mutiny and the roles of William Bligh and Fletcher Christian).

Barker, Ralph, *Against the Sea*. New York: St Martin's, 1972.

Baker, Daniel B. (ed.) *Explorers and Discoverers of the World*. Washington DC: Gale Research, Inc., 1993.

Baker, J. N. L., *A History of Geographical Exploration and Discovery*. New York: Houghton-Mifflin, 1931.

Bedini, Silvio A. (ed.) *The Christopher Columbus Encyclopedia*. Vols I and II. New York: Simon & Schuster, 1992.

Bendheim, Joan Tindale (translator) *Vinland the Good: The Saga of Leif Eriksson and the Discovery of America*. Norway: Fabritus & Sonners, 1970.

Black, Jeremy, *Maps and History: Constructing Images of the Past*. New York: Yale University Press, 1997.

Bohlander, Richard E. (ed.) *World Explorers and Discoverers*. New York: Macmillan, 1992.

Borne, Russell, *The Big Golden Book of Christopher Columbus and Other Early Adventurers*. New York: Western, 1991.

Brown, Lloyd A., *The Story of Maps*. New York: Dover, 1979.

Cary, Max and Warmington, E. H., *The Ancient Explorers*. London: Methuen, 1929.

Civardi, Anne and Graham-Campbell, James, *The Time Traveler Book of Viking Raiders*. Osborne, 1977.

Cordingly, David, *Under the Black Flag: The Romance and the Reality of Life Among the Pirates*. New York: Random House, 1995 (Scholarly and authoritative – but entertaining).

Crone, G. R., *Maps and Their Makers*. London: Hutchinson University Library, 1962.

Deacon, G. E. R. (ed.) *Seas, Maps, and Man: An Atlas History of Man's Exploration of the Oceans*. New York: Crescent Books, 1972.

Delpar, Helen (ed.) *The Discoverers: An Encyclopedia of Explorers and Exploration*. New York: McGraw-Hill, 1980.

Dodge, Stephen C., *Christopher Columbus and the First Voyages to the New World*. New York: Chelsea House, 1991.

Dor-Ner, Zvi and Scheller, William, *Columbus and the Age of Discovery*. New York: William Morrow, 1991.

Dunn, Oliver and Kelley, James E. Jr. (translators) *The Diary of Christopher Columbus's First Voyage to America 1492–1493*. University of Oklahoma Press, 1989.

Everett, Felicity and Reed, Struan, *The Usborne Book of Explorers, From Columbus to Armstrong*. England: Usborne, 1991.

Frith, Henry, *The Romance of Navigation: A Brief Record of Maritime Discovery*. London: Ward Lock & Bowden, 1893.

Goodnough, David, *John Cabot and Son*. New Jersey: Troll Associates, 1979.

Grant, Neil, *The Discoverers: The Living Past*. New York: Arco, 1979–1984.

Hargrove, Jim. *The World's Great Explorers: Ferdinand Magellan*. Chicago: Children's Press, 1990.

Harley, J. D. and Woodward, D., *A History of Cartography: Cartography in Prehistoric, Ancient and Medieval Europe and the Mediterranean*. University of Chicago Press. Volume I 1987; Volume II 1993.

Harley, Ruth, *Captain James Cook*. New Jersey: Troll Associates, 1979.

Harley, Ruth, *Ferdinand Magellan: Adventures in Discovery*. New Jersey: Troll Associates, 1979.

Harley, Ruth, *Henry Hudson*. New Jersey: Troll Associates, 1979.

Hills, Ken, *The Voyage of Columbus*. New York: Random House, 1991.

Hodgkiss, Alan G., *Discovering Antique Maps*. Buckinghamshire, UK: Shire, 1971.

Hourani, George Faldo, *Arab Seafaring in the Indian Ocean*. Princeton: Princeton University Press, 1951.

Howse, Derek and Sanderson, Michael, *The Sea Chart*. New York: McGraw-Hill, 1973.

Jobé, J. *The Great Age of Sail*. 1977.

June, Cecil (ed.) *The Four Voyages of Columbus*. New York: Dover, 1988.

Kent, Zachery, *The World's Great Explorers: James Cook*. Chicago: Children's Press, 1991.

Konstam, Angus, *A Historical Atlas of Exploration, 1492–1600*. New York: Checkmark Books, 2000 (Excellent maps of each major voyage and descriptions of explorations).

Lane, Christopher with Cresswell, Donald, *A Guide to Collecting Antique Maps*. Philadelphia, PA: The Philadelphia Print Shop, 1997.

Levathes, Louise, *When China Ruled the Seas: The Treasure Fleet of the Dragon Throne*. New York: Simon & Schuster, 1994.

McIntosh, Gregory (ed.) *Antique Map Reproductions*. Lakewood, CA: Plus Ultra, 1998.

Mollat du Mourdin. M. et. al., *Sea Charts of the Early Explorers*. London: Thames & Hudson, 1984.

Moreland, Carl and Bannister, David, *Antique Maps*. London: Longman, 1985; third edition, Phaidon, 1989.

Moscati, Sabatino (ed.) *The Phoenicians*. New York: Abbeville, 1988.

Newby, E, *World Atlas of Exploration*. New York: Crescent Books, 1975.

Place, Robin, *The Vikings, Fact and Fiction: Adventures of Young Vikings in Jorvik*. Cambridge: Cambridge University Press, 1987.

Price, A. Grenfell, *The Explorations of Captain James Cook in the Pacific, As Told by Selections of His Own Journals 1768–1779*. New York: Dover, 1971.

Ronciéré, Monique de la., *I Portolani: Carte nautiche dal XIII al XVII secolo*. Bramante Arte, 1992 (All portolani in this book are examined in de la Ronciéré's magnificent work).

Ryan, Peter, *Time Detectives: Explorers and Mapmakers*. London: Belitha Press, 1989.

Shirley, Rodney W., *The Mapping of the World*. London: Holland Press, 1983.

Simon, Charnan, *The World's Great Explorers: Leif Eriksson and the Vikings*. Chicago: Children's Press, 1991.

Skelton, R.A., *Decoratively Printed Maps of the 15th to 18th Centuries*, London: Spring Books, 1965 (Based on a 1926 book by A. L. Humphreys).

Starkey, Dinah, *A Scholastic Atlas of Exploration*. New York: HarperCollins, 1993.

Stefiff, Rebecca, *Ferdinand Magellan and the Discovery of the World Ocean*. New York: Chelsea House, 1990.

Sullivan, George, *Slave Ship: The Story of the Henrietta Marie*. New York: Cobblehill, 1994 (For children, but is informative for adults also).

Sullivan, George, *Discover Archaeology. An Introduction to the Tools and Techniques of Archeological* Fieldwork. New York: Doubleday, 1980.

Thomas, Lowell, *The Untold Story of Exploration*. New York: Dodd Mead, 1935.

Tooley, R.V., Bricker, C. and Crone, G. R., *Landmarks of Mapmaking*. Amsterdam, Brussels, 1968 (In other editions known as *A History of Cartography*).

Whitfield, Peter, *New Found Lands: Maps in the History of Exploration*. London: The British Library, 1998.

Whitfield, Peter, *The Charting of the Oceans: Ten Centuries of Maritime Maps*. Pomegranate, 1996.

Wigal, Donald, 'Leonardo da Vinci', and 'Jules Verne', in *The Visions of Nostradamus and Other Prophets*. New York: Random House, 1999.

Williams, J. E. D., *Sails to Satellites: The Origins and Development of Navigational Science*. Oxford: Oxford University Press, 1992.

THE HISTORY OF EARLY NAVAL ARCHITECTURE

Histories of naval architecture often begin with descriptions of log rafts and canoes, then vessels by the Phoenicians, Greeks, Romans, Africans, and eventually the magnificent sailing ships of the Spanish, Portuguese, British, and Americans. That was the approach of John Fincham's overview in his 1851 *A History of Naval Architecture*, Scoular Press, London, 1979 reprint.

A similar approach, only limited to northern Europe, is presented in George Bochmen's Prehistoric Naval Architecture, National Museum, London, 1891. In an even earlier text, David Steel in 1805 identified the principles established in Great Britain on shipbuilding in *The Elements and Practice of Naval Architecture*, W. Simpkin & R. Marshall, London, 1822. It describes the principles and practice of constructing ships for the Royal and mercantile navies.

Serious students of naval history also study related classics, such as *A Text-Book of Naval Architecture for the Use of Officers of the Royal Navy*, the British naval manual issued in 1889.

A standard textbook on actual naval architecture rather than on only its history is Henry Rossell's *Principles of Naval Architecture, The Society of Naval Architects and Marine Engineers*, New York, 1939; 12th printing, 1962.

For an appreciation of progress during the 20th century, students can compare Rossell with Edward Attwood's *Text-Book of Theoretical Naval Architecture*, Longmans Green, London, 1917, 7th edition). Students of naval architecture also study independent practical works, such as the treatise by Jean Boudriot, *The Seventy-Four Gun Ship*, Paris, 1986 reprint, translated from the French *Collection Archéologie Navale Française*, 1973.

Texts currently in use include *Applied Naval Architecture*, by Robert Zubaly, Cornell Maritime Press, 1996, and *Intoduction to Naval Architecture* by Thomas Gillmer (US Naval Institute, 1982).

Videos

The August F. Crabtree Collection of Miniature Ships. The Mariners' Museum, 1996. Actual shipbuilding techniques are demonstrated by this master of model-making.

The Art of the Ship Modeler shows in detail 19 models from The Mariners' Museum's collection. It was produced by the museum in 1996.

The Great Ships: Navigation. High Tech. High Seas. The History Channel.

Napoleon's Lost Fleet. The Discovery Channel.

Articles

James, Geoffrey, 'New Found Land', *New York Times Magazine*, September 19, 1999; page 70.

Ganson, Arthur, 'Making Time', *New York Times Magazine*, September 19, 1999; page 76.

Starn, Doug et Mike, 'Great Leap Forward', *New York Times Magazine*, September 19, 1999; page 78.

Chalmers, Catherine, 'Hello, Columbus', *New York Times Magazine*, September 19, 1999; page 87.

LaChapelle, David, 'The Drug Wars', *New York Times Magazine*, September 19, 1999; page 104.

Author's Acknowledgements

Antoni Bautista; Brown University Library; Stephany Evans for heroic patience and expert editing; William Kuhns for the use of his library and continual support; The Mariners' Museum, Newport News, Virginia; Harry Mushenheim, University of Dayton; Kay O'Reilly; George Sullivan; Craig Zraly and the libraries of Columbia University and Barnard College. For translations: Linda Busacca, *ringrazlamenti*; Vera Haldy, *danke schön*; Yvone Sanfir, *merci beaucoup*; Marina Montoya, *grazias*.

Donald Wigal, July 4, 2000

LIST OF ILLUSTRATIONS

A

Aegean Sea, 1500 (?).	52
Aegean Sea, 1624	164
The American Explorer Frederick Cook Planting the United-States Flag in North Pole, 12 September 1909.	228
Amoy Bay, 1699.	198
Arab Map Featuring Arabia as the Centre of the World, 10th century.	10
The Arrival of Hernán Cortés in Mexico, 16th century.	120
The Artist's Studio, c. 1665.	6
Atlantic Ocean, 1513.	72
Atlantic Ocean, 1534.	96-97
Atlantic Ocean, 1550.	112
Atlantic Ocean, 1601.	150
Atlantic Ocean, 1613.	159
Atlantic Ocean, 1618.	162
Atlantic Ocean, after 1549 (c. 1550).	111
Atlantic Ocean and Mediterranean Sea, 1563.	134
Atlantic Ocean, Mediterranean Sea and Black Sea, 1462.	45
Atlantic Ocean, Mediterranean Sea and Black Sea, 1603.	153
Atlas, c. 1630.	172-173
Atlas (Aegean Sea and Crete), 1313.	14
Atlas (Atlantic Ocean from Denmark to Malaga), 1467.	49
Atlas (Atlantic Ocean from Spain to Cape Verde), 1467.	47
Atlas (Black Sea), 1313.	12
Atlas (Black Sea), 1559.	127
Atlas (Central Mediterranean Sea), 1313.	13
Atlas (Cyprus Isle), 1587.	146
Atlas (French, English and Irish Coasts), c. 1321.	18
Atlas (Occidental Europe), 1559.	125
Atlas (Oriental Atlantic and Occidental Mediterranean), 1559.	126
Atlas (Oriental India and Japan), 1571.	136
Atlas (Peru Coasts), c. 1630.	176
Atlas (South America), 1583.	145
Atlas (South East Asia), 1587.	147
Atlas (Spanish Coasts), c. 1321.	20-21
Atlas of the Mediterranean, 1620.	160-161
Aztec Prince in Ceremonial Dress, 1579.	129

B

La Baie de la Table, 1686.	91
The Banda Islands, c. 1690.	194-195
Bartolomé de Las Casas (detail).	77
The Battle of Lepanto, 7 October 1571.	148-149
The Battle of Tepeaca, 16th century.	121
The Boke of Idrography (Atlantic Ocean), 1542.	98
The Boke of Idrography (Oriental India), 1542.	94
Brazil, 1579.	139

C

Cantino's Planisphere, 1502.	67
Captain James Cook, 1775-1776.	201
Cast Silver Plaque Depicting the Voyage of Sir Francis Drake, 1589.	144
Catalan Atlas (Atlantic Ocean and Western Mediterranean Sea), c. 1375.	28
Christopher Columbus Presenting the New World Treasures to the Souverains of Spain.	61
The 'Christopher Columbus' Map, c. 1492.	57
The Coast of North West Java, 1688.	193
Compass Dial, 18th century.	64
Complete Map of All Nations, c. 1620.	202-203
Conversation in the Franciscan Monastery of Santa Maria de La Rabida between the Navigator Christopher Columbus, the Physician Garcia Fernandez, the Priest Juan Perez and Alonzo Pinzón (detail).	58
Cook Landing at Tanna, One of the New Hebrides, c. 1775-1776.	210-211
Copy of the Map of Tenochtitlán, by Hernán Cortés (1485-1547), 1524.	128
Critical Position of H.M.S. Investigator on the North-Coast of Baring Island, 20 August 1851, 1854.	225
Cynoramphus Zealandicus, Black-Fronted Parakeet and *Cochlospermum Gillivraei, Kapok Tree*.	204

D
Departure of the Santa Maria, the Pinta and the Niña from Palos in 1492. — 68
Description of New France, 1607. — 158

F
Facsimile of the letter left by the Franklin expedition that notes where they abandoned the ships and the death of Franklin, 1859. — 229
Francisco Pizarro, Sailor and Conquistador, 1835. — 100
The Friendly Islands, 1798. — 221
From the Baltic Sea to the Niger, 1413. — 33
From the Baltic Sea to the Red Sea, 1339. — 26

G / H
Globe, 1492 (1847, copy). — 50-51
Greek Coasts, 1500 (?). — 55
The Hudson and Davis Straits, before 1677. — 189

I
Ile-de-Bréhat, 1666. — 187
Illustration from *Journal of Discovery of the Sources of the Nile,* 1863. — 78
Illustration from the *Voyage de Gouin de Beauchesne,* 1698-1701. — 74, 75
Indian Ocean, 1634. — 179
Indian Ocean, 1660. — 182
Indian Ocean, 1665. — 185

J
Jacques Cartier Discovering the Saint Laurent River in Canada in 1535, 1847. — 114-115
The Japanese Archipelago, 1625. — 166
John Harrison's Marine Chronometer Number 1 (H1), 1730-1735. — 64

K
Kitab-i-Bahriye ('The Book of the Seafarers') (Coast of Asia Minor), 1525-1526. — 89
Kitab-i-Bahriye ('The Book of the Seafarers') (Crete), 1525-1526. — 88

L
The Last Mile of Livingstone, in *The Life and Explorations of Dr David Livingstone,* 1878. — 79
The Last Voyage of Henry Hudson, 1881. — 174
Liber Insularum Archipelagi (Chios), 1420. — 37
Liber Insularum Archipelagi (Corfu), 1420. — 36
Louis XVI Giving Instructions to the Captain La Pérouse, for his Voyage of Exploration Around the World in the Presence of the Marquis de Castries, Ministry of the Navy, 29 June 1785, 1817. — 216-217

M
The Madagascar Roadstead, 1660. — 183
A Man of the Sandwich Islands in a Mask, 1784. — 209
Map of Japan from the Indian Ocean, c. 1613. — 156-157
Map of New Holland (Australia) and New Guinea, 1798. — 218
Map of New Zealand, 1798. — 208
Map of the Island of Newfoundland, 1689. — 193
Map of the Major Maritime Explorations. — 238-239
Map of the New Hebrides (now called Vanuatu) and New Caledonia, 1798. — 200
Map of the Port-des-Français, 1797. — 215
Marco Polo, 1857. — 27
Marco Polo Leaves Venice on his Famous Journey to the Far East, c. 1400. — 39
Marco Polo with Elephants and Camels Arriving at Hormuz on the Gulf of Persia from India, early 15th century. — 40-41
Martin Frobisher, 1570's. — 151
The Mediterranean Basin, 1565. — 135
Mediterranean Sea, 1422. — 48
Mediterranean Sea, 1662. — 184
Mediterranean Sea, c. 1385. — 29
Mediterranean Sea, c. 1600-1610. — 152
Mediterranean Sea and Black Sea, 1409. — 31
Mediterranean Sea and Black Sea, 1447. — 44
The Miller Atlas (Arabia and India), c. 1519. — 80
The Miller Atlas (Atlantic), c. 1519. — 86-87
The Miller Atlas (Brazil), c. 1519. — 84
The Miller Atlas (Madagascar), c. 1519. — 76
The Miller Atlas (Malaysia, Sumatra), c. 1519. — 83
The Miller Atlas (The Azores), c. 1519. — 73
Mocha, 1683. — 190-191
The Monomotapa Empire, 1677. — 188

N

Nautical Guide to France (Description hydrographique de la France), 1628. — 165
Nautical World Map, 1634. — 180
Naval Steerage. — 103
Nicolas Kratzer, 1528. — 17
Nordenskiöld's Ships, The Vega and Lena Saluting the Cape Chelyuskin, 19 August 1878. — 222
North Atlantic Ocean, 1674. — 186
North Atlantic Ocean, c. 1628. — 169
North Eastern Atlantic Ocean, Mediterranean Sea and Eastern Black Sea, c. 1610. — 155
The Northern Ocean, 1628. — 170

O

Octant, c. 1750. — 64
Orbis Typus Universalis Iuxta Hydrographorum Traditionem Exactissime Depicta, 1522. — 34
Oseberg Ship, c. 817. — 23

P

Pacific Ocean, 1622. — 167
Pacific Ocean, 1649. — 181
Persian/Arabian Gulf, 1699. — 196-197
Phaethon Rubricauda, Redtailed Tropicbird. — 205
Pilot Manual for the Use of Breton Mariners (Atlantic Maps), 1548. — 107
Pilot Manual for the Use of Breton Mariners (Quadrante of the Drizzles, Le Havre to Mores Maps), 1548. — 108
The Pisana Map, 1290. — 9
Plan of the Endeavour. — 213
Planisphere, c. 1505. — 62-63
Polar Dress and Eskimo's Eyewear. — 224
Portolano of Dijon, c. 1510. — 71
Portrait of Abel Tasman, his Wife and Daughter, 1637. — 175
Portrait of Bartolomeu Dias. — 81
Portrait of Captain James Clarke Ross. — 214
Portrait of Christopher Columbus, first half of the 16th century. — 59
Portrait of Ferdinand Magellan. — 105
Portrait of Hernán Cortés. — 116
Portrait of John Cabot (Giovanni Caboto), 1455 (?)-1498. — 56
Portuguese Map of the World (Cyprus), c. 1585. — 142-143
Provençal Atlas of the Mediterranean, 1633. — 177

R

Rigged Model of a Portuguese Caravela from c.1535. — 102
Rio de Janeiro Bay, 1579. — 140

S

The Sandwich Islands (Later Known as the Hawaiian Islands), 1798. — 206-207
The Sea, 1864. — 226-227
Seascape, Moonlight, 1878. — 237
Sir John Franklin, c. 1830. — 219
Sled Dogs Sitting on the Snow at the South Pole, 14 December 1911, 1911. — 231
Snow, Storm. Steam-Boat off a Harbour's Mouth, 1842. — 234

T

Tasman's Ship in Tonga. — 178
Tribes of Danes Crossing the Sea to Britain, 1125-1135. — 25

U / V

Universa ac navigabilis totius terrarum orbis descriptio, 1559. — 130-131
Venetian Atlas (Western Mediterranean Basin, Portugal, Spain and Western France), c. 1390. — 32
Viking Nave and Marine Monster, 12th century. — 22

W

The World (Florida), 1556. — 117
The World (Java), 1556. — 122
The World (Terra Nova), 1556. — 119
The World (The New France), 1556. — 118
World Map, 1500. — 54
World Map, 1529. — 92-93
World Map, 1534. — 104
World Map, 1543. — 101
World Map, 1550. — 113
World Map, 1566. — 133
World Map, after 1262. — 11
World Map (detail), 1375. — 42

www.ingramcontent.com/pod-product-compliance
Lightning Source LLC
Chambersburg PA
CBHW042040200426
43209CB00060B/1707